Table of Con

Introduction

Thank you for purchasing this study guide for the Certification Foundation examination administered by the International Association of Privacy Professionals ("IAPP"). By purchasing this guide, you have taken the first step to passing the exam and becoming a certified privacy professional!

Before you begin working your way through this guide, you should be aware of how it is organized. This guide begins with a condensed text covering core privacy principles, which is then followed by an extensive set of sample questions with detailed answers. Although working through sample questions is the best way to study for the exam, you will also need a thorough understanding of core privacy principles to pass the exam. This guide provides you with both. The introductory text portion provides you with the fundamentals, while the sample questions and answers reinforce and supplement your knowledge.

Each chapter of this guide begins with a list of important terms relevant to the subject matter addressed in that chapter. Definitions of the terms can be found in the IAPP's glossary. You should read the definition provided for each term several times. Many questions on the exam come directly from the glossary, and therefore it is important to thoroughly understand the listed terms. The glossary is located at:

http://www.cippexam.com/glossary

Finally, please remember to carefully read the sample questions and answers provided at the end of this guide. In some cases, the sample questions test subject matter not fully disclosed in the condensed text portion of this guide. In these cases, the questions are designed to supplement the material contained in the text. It is therefore important that you read the questions and answers several times so that you completely understand the concepts tested.

By systematically working your way through this guide, you will have all the information necessary to pass the exam on your very first try!

About the Certification Foundation Examination

The Certification Foundation examination is the gateway to all of IAPP's certifications. The exam covers the fundamental principles of information privacy and protection from a global perspective. To receive a certification from the IAPP, a candidate must successfully pass the Certification Foundation exam and one other specialty exam, including CIPP/US, CIPP/C, CIPP/E, CIPP/G, CIPP/IT, and CIPM.

The Certification Foundation exam is a 90 minute, 90 item, objective (i.e., multiple-choice) test. There are no essay questions, and each correct answer is worth one point. You are not penalized for incorrect answers. Therefore, a general exam taking strategy is to answer every question on the exam, even those you are unsure of. Eliminate obviously incorrect answers and then choose the best answer remaining. Do not leave any questions unanswered.

Finally, on a more personal note, be sure to give yourself adequate time to prepare for the examination. This guide is quite lengthy, and you will need several weeks (at a minimum) to work through all of the material. Take your time and absorb the material. You will not obtain a firm grasp of the information contained in this guide by simply skimming it. Carefully read the sample questions as well as the detailed answers. You will likely see dozens of questions on your exam that test the same subject matter as our sample questions. If you answer these questions correctly, you are well on your way to becoming certified privacy professional.

Good Luck!

Chapter 1: Fundamental Privacy Principles

This chapter addresses common themes and principles to information privacy in the United States and overseas. You should expect anywhere from 31 to 35 questions on your examination testing subject matter covered in this chapter.

A. Glossary Terms

It is important that you thoroughly understand fundamental privacy principles before taking the exam because of the relatively high number of questions testing the fundamentals. Therefore, you should carefully read the definitions provided in the glossary for the important terms listed below. The glossary is located at:

http://www.cippexam.com/glossary

Glossary Terms: Accountability, APEC Privacy Principles, Bodily Privacy, Choice, Closed Circuit Television, Collection Limitation, Communications Privacy, Consent, Customer Information, Data Controller, Data Elements, Data Processor, Data Protection Directive, Data Quality, Data Subject, De-identification, European Convention for the Protection of Human Rights and Fundamental Freedoms, Fair Credit Reporting Act, Fair Information Practices, Four Classes of Privacy, Individual Participation, Information Lifecycle, Information Privacy, International Data Transfers, Internet Protocol Address, Internet Service Provider, Jurisdiction, Madrid Resolution, Minimum Necessary Requirement, Negligence, OECD Guidelines, Openness, Opt-in, Opt-out, Organization for Economic Cooperation and Development, Personal Data, Personal Information, Privacy Assessment, Privacy by Design, Privacy Impact Assessment, Privacy Notice, Privacy Policy, Public Records, Publicly Available Information, Purpose Specification, Retention, Right to Privacy, Security Safeguards, Special Categories of Data, Territorial Privacy, Universal Declaration of Human Rights, Use Limitation.

B. Definition of Privacy

Privacy has been defined in many ways. For example, some view privacy as the fundamental right to be left alone. Others define privacy as the right of an individual to be protected against intrusion into his personal life or affairs by direct physical means or by publication of information.

In general, all definitions of privacy revolve around the notion that society should respect an individual's autonomy, and an individual should be free from unreasonable intrusion on that autonomy from both the government and private parties. No matter how one defines privacy, there remains a universal and almost innate understanding of the importance of privacy and privacy protection. Accordingly, many diverse regions and cultures today recognize privacy rights.

C. Types of Privacy

Privacy can be divided into four main types or areas, as shown in Figure 1 on the next page. Each type is related, but a separate and distinct framework has developed for analyzing each area. The four types of privacy are:

1. Information privacy: concerned with the collection and handling of personal data, such as credit information and medical records. The focus of the Certification Foundation exam is on principles associated with information privacy.

2. Bodily privacy: involves protection of an individual's physical being and includes issues such as genetic testing and drug testing.

3. Communication privacy: encompasses the security and confidentiality of all types of correspondence, including email, postal mail, telephone and fax communications, as well as ordinary verbal communications.

4. Territorial privacy: concerned with intrusion into an individual's environment (e.g., home, workplace) and addresses issues such as video surveillance and identification checks.

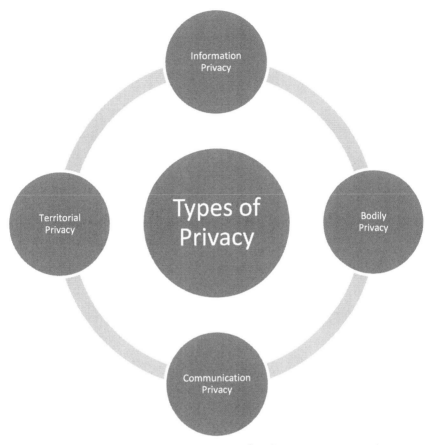

Figure 1: Types of Privacy

D. Types of Information

For privacy purposes, all information can be classified as either (1) personal information or (2) non-personal information. Personal information has been given different labels across the globe. For example, countries in the European Union ("EU") generally use the term "personal data" to describe personal information. In the United States, the term "personally identifiable information" (or "PII") is typically used. Canada simply uses "personal information" in its core privacy law, which is titled Personal Information Protection and Electronic Documents Act ("PIPEDA"). The meaning of the term, regardless of which label is used, is generally the same. Personal information is any information (i.e., both paper and electronic records) that relates to or describes an _identified or identifiable individual_. Accordingly, information about a corporation is not generally considered personal information because it does not relate to an individual.

The dividing line between personal and non-personal information is sometimes blurred. For example, a specific job title may uniquely identify a person (e.g., chief executive officer). However, some titles are not very specific (e.g., associate) and may apply to hundreds, if not thousands, of people at an organization. When determining whether information is personal, a good rule of thumb is to determine how uniquely the information describes a person. Information that is unique to a specific person or small group of persons is more likely to constitute personal information. Applying this principle, the human resources data elements "department" and "title" may not be considered personal because they relate to a potentially large group of people. In contrast, "salary" and other more uniquely identifying data, such as performance evaluations, would generally constitute personal data.

Certain types of important personal information may be further classified as "sensitive" data. What constitutes sensitive data differs from one jurisdiction to another. For example, Article 8 of the EU Data Protection Directive defines sensitive data, which is called "special categories of data," as information that reveals racial origin, political opinions, religious or philosophical beliefs, trade-union membership, or data concerning health or sex life. In the United States, social security numbers are generally considered sensitive. In virtually all jurisdictions, health related data, such as prescribed medications and medical diagnoses, constitutes sensitive person information because it relates to the inner workings of one's body and mind, which is inherently personal and private.

Non-personal information is all data that does not relate to an identified or identifiable individual. For example, data that has been "anonymized," "de-identified" or "aggregated" for research or statistical purposes constitutes non-personal information.

E. Sources of Personal Information

There are three main sources of personal information. They include:

1. Public records: information collected and maintained by the government and available to the public. Example of public records include real estate deeds, birth and marriage certificates, tax liens, and other data recorded by the government and made available for public inspection.

2. Publicly available information: information, in any form, that is generally accessible to the interested public. Examples of publicly available information include information contained in newspapers, research articles, books and other publications, as well as information obtained through Internet searches.

3. Non-public information: information that has not been made available to the general public. Examples of non-public information include a company's trade secrets, as well as business plans and strategy related documents.

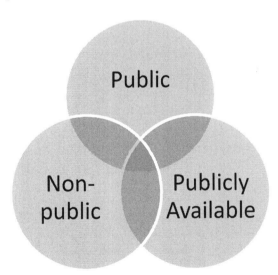

Figure 2: Sources of Information

As shown in Figure 2, information may be derived from more than one of these sources. For example, a public company's financial data is generally non-public information before an earnings call, publicly available information after an earnings call or press release containing the information, and a public record once it is formally included as part of a Securities and Exchange Commission ("SEC") report. It is important to consider the source of the information because it dictates how the information may be used. For example, personal data obtained from public records can generally be used without restriction, whereas personal data obtained from non-public sources typically cannot be used unless permission is obtained.

For the most part, privacy laws only protect activities relating to personal information. In other words, privacy laws typically do not protect non-personal information. Therefore, a preliminary question that must be answered is whether an activity is performed on or with personal information. If personal information is involved, then various legal, regulatory, and contractual provisions may govern the activity. If the activity involves solely non-personal information, then it generally is outside the scope of privacy law. Accordingly, the threshold question of what constitutes personal information is a very important issue for privacy professionals. A plethora of legal right and obligations will attach to activities involving personal information, as explained later in this guide.

F. Entities that Process Personal Information

Most privacy laws regulate the "processing" of personal information. Virtually any activity performed on or with personal information is considered processing. Examples of processing include collection, recording, organization, storage, alteration, retrieval, consultation, use, disclosure, dissemination, blocking, erasure or destruction. Processing also encompasses both manual and automated means of performing these activities.

Three main parties are typically involved in the processing of personal information. They include:

1. Data controller: the person or entity that determines, alone or jointly with others, the purposes and the means of the processing of personal data.

2. Data processor: the person or entity that processes personal data on behalf of the controller.

3. <u>Data subject</u>: the person about whom the personal data relates to or describes.

For example, if a hospital collects personal information about its patients and transfers the personal information to a third-party that bills the patients, the hospital is the data controller, the biller is the data processor, and the patient is the data subject.

A fourth party may sometimes be involved in the processing of personal information. For example, personal data may be imported to or exported from a particular country. In this case, the data importer or exporter may have certain rights and obligations under the applicable laws of the importing or exporting countries. Therefore, the data importer or exporter may be a fourth party involved in the processing of personal information.

G. Privacy Policies and Notices

Although many people use the terms "privacy policy" and "privacy notice" interchangeably, they actually represent two distinct statements.

A <u>privacy policy</u> is an internal statement that describes an organization's information handling practices and procedures. It is directed to the employees and agents of the organization.

A <u>privacy notice</u>, on the other hand, is an external statement that is directed to an organization's prospective and actual customers or users. It describes how the organization will process personal information. The privacy notice also typically describes the options a data subject has with respect to the organization's processing of his personal information (e.g., the opportunity to "opt-out"). It is common for an organization to use its privacy policy as a privacy notice. For example, an organization may publish its privacy notice on its website and rebrand the notice as a privacy policy.

The distinction between a privacy policy and a private notice is often tested on the Certification Foundation exam. In addition, many incorrect answers on the exam will use these terms incorrectly. For example, if an answer choice implies that a privacy policy is used as an external statement to inform customers about an organization's privacy practices, it is not likely the correct answer. On the exam, "privacy policy" and "private notice" represent two distinct statements. Again, a privacy policy is an internal statement, while a privacy notice is an external statement. This makes intuitive sense because policies are generally internal operating documents, while notices are typically external announcements.

H. Data Controls and Risk Assessment

Generally, there are three types of controls or safeguards that an organization may use to manage and protect personal information. They include:

1. <u>Administrative</u>: management related policies or procedures for protecting personal information. An incident management plan and a privacy policy are two examples of administrative controls.

2. <u>Physical</u>: controls that physically protect or prevent access to a resource. Examples of physical controls include cable locks for laptops and security guards for preventing unauthorized access to a building.

3. <u>Technical</u>: measures that utilize technology to protect personal information. Examples of technical controls include password authentication schemes, encryption, and smart cards.

Managing risk associated with the processing of personal information is an important responsibility of an organization. Several tools exist to help an organization manage its data processing risk.

A <u>privacy impact assessment</u> ("PIA") is a systematic process for identifying the potential privacy related implications of a proposed system. When conducting a PIA, an organization analyzes how information is collected, stored, protected, shared and managed to ensure that an organization has consciously incorporated privacy protection throughout the entire lifecycle of the data. A PIA should be carried out whenever a new system or project is proposed, or when revisions to existing practices are planned. A PIA should also be performed when (1) an organization is introducing a new information technology system for storing and accessing personal information, (2) planning to participate in a new data sharing initiative with another organization, or (3) intending to use existing data for a new and potentially more intrusive purpose.

A privacy audit or assessment is a systematic examination of an organization's compliance with its privacy policy and procedures, applicable law and regulations, and other agreements and contracts concerning personal information. Audits should be conducted on a regular basis or at the request of a regulatory authority. Typically, privacy audits are performed by an internal task force of employees. However, when internal auditors are responsible for developing and implementing a privacy program, their independence may be impaired. For this reason, and due to the need for technical and legal expertise, third-party auditors may be used.

Both privacy impact assessments and privacy audits are important tools that organizations should regularly use to manage their privacy related risk.

I. The Information Lifecycle

All information, including personal information, undergoes a lifecycle at an organization. It is important to understand this lifecycle when developing a privacy policy that protects personal data throughout the various stages of its existence at an organization. As shown in Figure 3 on the next page, the data lifecycle consists of (1) collection, (2) use, (3) disclosure, and (4) retention or destruction.

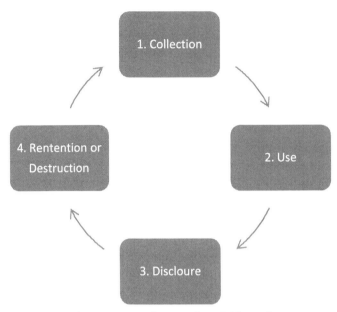

Figure 3: Information Lifecycle

A privacy policy should address an organization's information handling practices and procedures throughout the entire lifecycle from collection to retention or destruction of the information.

J. Fair Information Principles

The Fair Information Principles ("FIPs") are guidelines that represent widely-accepted doctrines concerning the fair processing of information. FIPs serve as the building block of many international privacy initiatives, most notably the Guidelines on the Protection of Privacy and Transborder Flows of Personal Data adopted by the Organization for Economic Cooperation and Development in 1980 ("OECD Guidelines").

The core principles of privacy addressed by the FIPs are:

1. <u>Notice and awareness</u>: Consumers should be given notice of an organization's information practices before any personal information is collected from them.

2. Choice and consent: Consumers should have options to control how their data is used.

3. Access and participation: Consumers should have the ability to view, verify, and contest the accuracy of data collected about them.

4. Integrity and security: Organizations that collect data should ensure that the collected data is accurate and secure.

5. Enforcement and redress: Enforcement measures, such as regulatory oversight with civil and/or criminal penalties for noncompliance, should be implemented to ensure that organizations follow the FIPs.

K. Types of Choice and Consent

There are two fundamental types of choice and consent that an organization may provide to a data subject. The first is called "opt-in" and the second is called "opt-out."

Opt-in consent occurs when a data subject affirmatively and explicitly indicates his desire to have his data processed by an organization. For example, when a data subject expressly tells a data processor that certain specified types of processing are allowed on his data, he is opting in to the specified processing. Opt-in consent is sometimes referred to as affirmative consent.

Opt-out consent, on the other hand, is when a data subject implicitly consents by not indicating his disapproval of the requested processing. For example, if a data processor tells a data subject that his data will be processed in a particular way unless he notifies the processor within ten days, the processor is providing the data subject with the opportunity to opt-out.

A good way to remember the difference between opt-in and opt-out consent is to consider what happens to a data subject's information if no action is taken. With opt-in consent, information is excluded from processing if the data subject does not act. With opt-out consent, information is included in processing if the data subject does not act.

In connection with online data processing, opt-in and opt-out consent can be illustrated with the use of the following web form.

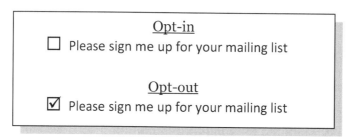

Figure 4: Opt-in and Opt-out Illustration

With opt-in consent, the data subject must affirmatively check the box in order to join the organization's mailing list. The default action is that the data subject will not be added to the organization's mailing list. With opt-out consent, the box is pre-checked, and the data subject will join the mailing list unless he unselects the box. Thus, the default action is inclusion on the mailing list.

As will be described later in this guide, some types of processing will require a data subject to affirmatively opt-in, while other types of processing require only opt-out consent. Opt-in consent is generally reserved for more intrusive processing, such as the transfer of sensitive personal information to third-parties, while opt-out consent is appropriate for less intrusive forms of processing, such as the sending of commercial emails to a recipient with an existing business relationship with the organization sending the commercial emails.

Chapter 2: World Models of Data Protection and Industry Specific Privacy Laws

This chapter addresses the major privacy regimes throughout the world and also privacy issues related to specific industries, such as the financial and healthcare industries. You should expect anywhere from 20 to 23 questions on your examination directed to subject matter from this chapter.

A. Glossary Terms

Your exam will contain a relatively high number of questions testing material from this chapter. Therefore, it is important that you read the definitions provided in the glossary for the terms listed below. The glossary is located at:

http://www.cippexam.com/glossary

Glossary Terms: Act Respecting the Protection of Personal Information in the Private Sector, Adequate Level of Protection, Article 29 Working Party, Background Screening / Checks, Binding Corporate Rules, Canadian Standards Association, Children's Online Privacy Protection Act of 2000, Commercial Activity, Comprehensive Laws, Cookie, Cookie Directive, Co-regulatory Model, Data Processing, Data Protection Authority, Data Protection Commissioner, Data Protection Directive, Direct Marketing, Do Not Track, Employee Information, Encryption, European Economic Area, EU-U.S. Safe Harbor Agreement, European Commission, European Union, Fair Credit Reporting Act, Federal Trade Commission, Freedom of Information Act, Gramm-Leach-Bliley Act, Health Information Technology for Economic and Clinical Heath Act, Health Insurance Portability and Accountability Act, Information Privacy, International Data Transfers, Medical Information, Non-public Personal information, PCI Data Security Standard, Personal Data, Personal Information, Personal Information Protection and Electronic Documents Act, Privacy Act of 1974, Public Records, Seal Programs, Sectoral Law / Model, Self-regulation Model, Smart Grid, Standard Model Clauses, Technology-based Model, WebTrust.

B. World Models of Privacy Protection

There are four major models of privacy protection used throughout the world. In most countries, several complementary models are employed simultaneously to effectively protect privacy rights of individuals. The four models are:

1. Comprehensive: In many countries, including those in the European Union ("EU"), there is a comprehensive or general law that governs the collection, use, and dissemination of personal information in both the private and public sectors. In countries employing a comprehensive model of privacy protection, an oversight body ensures compliance with the general privacy law. For example, each country in the EU has a national data protection authority responsible for ensuring compliance with the country's general privacy law, which is modeled after the EU Data Protection Directive.

2. Co-regulatory: A variant of the comprehensive model in which specific industries develop rules for the protection of privacy within that industry that are enforced by the industry and overseen by a privacy agency. Canada, Australia, and New Zealand are three countries employing a co-regulatory model of privacy protection.

3. Sectoral: Some countries, including the United States and Japan, enact sector specific laws instead of a general data protection law. In these countries, enforcement is achieved through various mechanisms, including regulatory bodies such as the Federal Trade Commission ("FTC") in the United States.

4. Self-regulatory: industry associations establish rules or regulations that are adhered to by industry participants. Examples include the Payment Card Industry Data Security Standard ("PCI DSS") and the privacy seal programs administered by the Online Privacy Alliance. An organization's privacy policy is also a form of self-regulation.

In addition to the four major models discussed above, technology plays an important role in privacy protection. For example, Internet users may employ a wide range of technologic measures, such as software programs and hardware systems, to protect their privacy. These include encryption, digital signatures, anonymous remailers, firewalls, and proxy servers. Chapter 3 of this guide more fully addresses Internet privacy principles.

C. Overview of Major Privacy Initiatives

As previously discussed, the OECD Guidelines were adopted in 1980. The OECD Guidelines set forth eight privacy principles derived partly from the fair information principles ("FIPs"). The eight principles are:

1. Collection Limitation Principle: There should be limits to the collection of personal data and any collected data should be obtained by lawful and fair means and, where appropriate, with the knowledge or consent of the data subject.

2. Data Quality Principle: Personal data should be relevant to the purpose for which it is to be used, and it should be accurate, complete and kept up-to-date.

3. Purpose Specification Principle: The purpose for which personal data is collected should be specified at or before the time of data collection, and subsequent use should be limited to the fulfillment of that purpose or compatible purposes.

4. Use Limitation Principle: Personal data should not be disclosed or used for purposes other than those specified, except when with the consent of the data subject or by the authority of law.

5. Security Safeguards Principle: Personal data should be protected by reasonable security safeguards against risk of loss or unauthorized access, destruction, use, modification or disclosure.

6. Openness Principle: There should be a general policy of candor about developments, practices, and policies with respect to personal data. Specifically, a data controller should be open and

honest about the existence and nature of collected personal data, as well as the identity and residence of the data controller.

7. Individual Participation Principle: An individual should have the right to (a) obtain from a data controller, or otherwise, confirmation of whether or not the data controller has data relating to him; (b) have communicated to him, data relating to him within a reasonable time; at a charge, if any, that is not excessive; in a reasonable manner; and in a form that is readily intelligible to him; (c) be given reasons if a request is denied, and to be able to challenge such denial; and (d) challenge the accuracy of data relating to him and, if the challenge is successful to have the data erased, rectified, completed or amended.

8. Accountability Principle: A data controller should be accountable for complying with measures that effectuate the principles stated above.

In 1995, the EU adopted Directive 95/46/EC ("EU Data Protection Directive"), which addressed the protection of individuals with regard to the processing of personal data and the free movement of personal data within the European Union. The right to privacy is a highly developed area of law in Europe where privacy is viewed as a fundamental right of all individuals.

The EU Data Protection Directive states that personal data should not be processed unless certain conditions are met. These conditions fall into three categories: (1) transparency, (2) legitimate purpose, and (3) proportionality. Each member state must also set up a supervisory authority, an independent body that will monitor the data protection level in that member state, give advice to the government about administrative measures and regulations, and start legal proceedings when the state's national data protection regulation has been violated.

In accordance with the EU Data Protection Directive, personal data may only be transferred to a country outside of the EU if that country provides an "adequate level of protection." Major countries that have been deemed adequate by the European Commission are

Andorra, Argentina, Canada, Iceland, Israel, Liechtenstein, Switzerland, and Uruguay.

If a country has not been deemed adequate (e.g., the United States), four options exist for transferring personal data out of the EU and to that country.

1. Model contracts have been drafted by the European Commission that when executed by an organization importing data from the EU ensure an adequate level of protection through contractual provisions in the model contracts.

2. Binding corporate rules ("BCRs") are internal rules (such as a Code of Conduct) adopted by a multinational group of related organizations which permit international transfers of personal data to related companies located in countries which do not provide an adequate level of protection. For example, if a German company has a subsidiary in the United States and the company desires to transfer personal data to its subsidiary, it may establish BCRs with its subsidiary that when approved by the German data protection authority, permit the transfer.

3. The U.S. Department of Commerce in consultation with the European Commission has developed a Safe Harbor program that permits the transfer of personal data out of the European Union to U.S. companies that have agreed to participate in the program.

4. The data subject may unambiguously consent to the transfer. Specifically, in accordance with the EU Data Protection Directive, the data subject may provide "any freely given specific and informed indication of his wishes" to have the data transferred.

All member states of the EU are also signatories of the European Convention on Human Rights ("ECHR"). Article 8 of the ECHR provides that every individual has "the right to respect for his private and family life, his home and his correspondence," subject to certain restrictions. In particular, any interference with an individual's right of privacy must be in accordance with law and necessary in a democratic society, in view of such public interests as national security and the prevention of crime.

In addition to the European Union, other regional organizations have adopted major privacy initiatives. In 2004, for example, the Asia-Pacific Economic Cooperation ("APEC") adopted a privacy system that is a self-regulatory code of conduct designed to create more consistent privacy protection for consumers when their data moves between countries with different privacy regimes in the APEC region. The FTC and the U.S. Department of Commerce helped develop the APEC privacy rules. In addition to the United States, the other APEC members include Australia, Brunei, Canada, Chile, China, Hong Kong, Indonesia, Japan, Korea, Malaysia, Mexico, New Zealand, Papua New Guinea, Peru, the Philippines, Russia, Singapore, Taiwan, Thailand, and Vietnam.

In 2009, over 80 countries adopted and approved the "Madrid Resolution" on international privacy. The purpose of the Madrid Resolution was twofold: (1) define a set of principles and rights guaranteeing the effective and internationally uniform protection of privacy and (2) facilitate of the international flow of personal data needed in a globalized world. In accordance with the Madrid Resolution, the data controller (referred to as the "responsible party") has a duty of confidentiality with respect to a data subject's personal data. In addition, the data controller must protect personal data with "appropriate technical and organizational measures to ensure ... their integrity, confidentiality and availability."

D. United States Federal Privacy Laws

For the Certification Foundation exam, you are expected to understand the basics of several United States laws that regulate the processing of personal information. As previously mentioned, the United States takes a sectoral approach to privacy protection, regulating specific industries with separate legislation.

Important federal laws regulating the private sector in the United States include the (1) Fair Credit Reporting Act ("FCRA"), (2) Gramm–Leach–Bliley Act ("GLBA"), (3) Health Insurance

Portability and Accountability Act ("HIPPA"), and (4) Children's Online Privacy Protection Act ("COPPA"). Important federal laws regulating the public sector include the (1) Privacy Act of 1974, and (2) Freedom of Information Act ("FOIA"). Each of these federal laws is discussed more fully below.

1. U.S. Laws Regulating the Private Sector

Let's begin with the two private sector federal laws that regulate the financial industry. The Fair Credit Reporting Act ("FRCA") was originally enacted in 1970 and was updated by the Fair and Accurate Credit Transactions Act of 2003 ("FACTA"). The FRCA applies to (1) consumer reporting agencies ("CRAs") (e.g., Experian, TransUnion, and Equifax) and (2) users of consumer reports. The purpose of the FCRA is to increase the accuracy and fairness of credit reporting and to limit the use of consumer reports to permissible purposes, such as for employment and the underwriting of insurance. The FRCA requires users of consumer reports to provide notice to the consumer, obtain consumer reports only for a permissible purpose, and provide certification of the user's permissible purpose to the CRA.

The Gramm–Leach–Bliley Act ("GLBA"), also known as the "Financial Services Modernization Act," was enacted in 1999. It applies to institutions that are significantly engaged in financial activities in the United States (also known as "domestic financial institutions"). The GLBA requires domestic financial institutions to, among other things, provide an initial privacy notice when the customer relationship is established and annually thereafter and provide an opt-out notice prior to sharing non-public personal information with unaffiliated third parties.

The next important federal law regulates the processing of personal information in the health care industry in the United States. The Health Insurance Portability and Accountability Act ("HIPAA") was enacted in 1996 to define policies, procedures and guidelines that covered entities must adhere to for maintaining the privacy and security of individually identifiable protected health information ("PHI"). Covered entities generally include health care clearinghouses, employer sponsored health plans, health insurers, and health care providers. As directed by Title II of HIPPA, the Department of Health and Human Services ("HHS") has promulgated two important rules to address the handling of PHI: (1) the Privacy Rule and (2) the Security Rule.

Under the Privacy Rule, covered entities may disclose PHI to facilitate treatment, payment, or health care operations without a patient's express written authorization. Any other disclosure of PHI requires the covered entity to obtain written authorization from the data subject for the disclosure. In addition, when a covered entity discloses PHI, it must make a reasonable effort to disclose only the _minimum necessary_ information required to achieve its purpose.

While the Privacy Rule pertains to all forms of PHI, including paper and electronic records, the Security Rule deals specifically with electronic Protected Health Information ("ePHI"). In accordance with the Security Rule, covered entities must implement three types of security safeguards to protect ePHI: (1) administrative, (2) physical, and (3) technical. For each of these types of safeguards, the Security Rule identifies various security standards, and for each standard, it provides both required and addressable implementation specifications.

The final private sector law regulating the processing of personal information is the Children's Online Privacy Protection Act ("COPPA"). COPPA was enacted in 1998 to curtail the collection of personal information from children. The Act applies to websites and online services operated for commercial purposes that are either directed to children under the age of 13 or have actual knowledge that children under the age of 13 are providing information online. In addition to requiring operators of these websites to conspicuously post a privacy notice, COPPA also requires that the website operator obtain verifiable parental consent prior to any collection, use, or disclosure of personal information from persons under the age of 13.

2. U.S. Laws Regulating the Public Sector

Now let's turn to the public sector laws. The Privacy Act of 1974 establishes fair information principles for the collection, maintenance, use, and dissemination of personally identifiable information that is maintained in systems operated by federal agencies. The Privacy Act prohibits the disclosure of information from a federally operated system of records absent the written consent of the data subject. The Act also provides individuals with a means by which to seek access to their records, and sets forth various agency record-keeping requirements.

The Freedom of Information Act ("FOIA") is a federal freedom of information law enacted in 1966 that allows for the full or partial disclosure of previously unreleased information and documents controlled by the United States government. FOIA defines agency records subject to disclosure, outlines mandatory disclosure procedures, and grants nine statutory exemptions to disclosure, such as federal records containing trade secrets.

Again, for the Certification Foundation exam, you are expected to understand only the basics of these federal laws. The CIPP/US exam goes into greater detail on each of these laws. If you are planning on taking the CIPP/US exam, be sure to read our study guide designed specifically for that exam.

Chapter 3: Internet Privacy

This chapter addresses privacy issues related to websites and other online activities. You should expect anywhere from 20 to 24 questions on your examination directed to subject matter from this chapter.

A. Glossary Terms

As previously mentioned, many questions on the exam will come directly from the definitions provided in the IAPP's glossary. Therefore, it is important that you read the definitions provided in the glossary for the terms listed below. The glossary is located at:

http://www.cippexam.com/glossary

Glossary Terms: Active Data Collection, Authentication, Behavioral Advertising, Caching, Children's Online Privacy Protection Act of 2000, Cookie, Cookie Directive, Cross-site Scripting, Cryptography, Customer Access, Encryption, Extensible Markup Language, Flash, Hyperlink, Hypertext Markup Language, Hypertext Transfer Protocol, Hypertext Transfer Protocol Secure, Internet Protocol Address, Internet Service Provider, JavaScript, Just-in-time Notification, Layered Notice, Location-based Service, Online Behavioral Advertising, Passive Data Collection, Phishing, Privacy by Design, Secure Sockets Layer, Social Engineering, SPAM, Stored Communications Act, Syndicated Content, Transmission Control Protocol, Transport Layer Security, Uniform Resource Locator, Web Beacon.

B. Overview of Internet Technologies

The Internet is a global system of interconnected computer networks that uses standard communications protocols to serve several billion users worldwide. It is a massive system that consists of millions of private, public, academic, business and government networks that are linked together by a broad array of electronic, wireless and optical networking technologies.

The two most prominent web technologies are Hypertext Transfer

Protocol ("HTTP") and Hypertext Markup Language ("HTML"). As its name suggests, HTTP is a protocol that facilitates the transfer of data on the Internet. Generally, an HTTP client sends a request message (e.g., a request for a webpage) to an HTTP server. The server, in turn, returns a response message (e.g., the requested webpage).

HTML is the main markup language for creating web pages and other information that can be displayed in a web browser. The language instructs a web browser how to render or display a webpage. A webpage written in HTML is accessed by an HTTP client through a unique Internet address called a uniform resource locator ("URL"). The URL is a specific character string that constitutes a reference to a resource. For example, http://www.cippexam.com is an example of a URL for a webpage that offers this guide for sale. A URL typically consists of a protocol identifier (e.g., "http") followed by a second-level domain (e.g., "cippexam.com") followed by a top-level domain (e.g., ".com"). Some URLs, as provided in the above example, include a sub-domain (e.g., "www").

Numerous other technologies are part of the Internet protocol suite. For example, transmission control protocol ("TCP") and Internet protocol ("IP") provide end-to-end connectivity for client and servers and specify how data should be formatted, addressed, transmitted, routed and received on the Internet.

In addition, there are two important security protocols used to protect information on the Internet. Transport layer security ("TLS") and its predecessor, secure sockets layer ("SSL"), are cryptographic protocols that provide secure communications over the Internet. Several versions of TLS and SSL are in widespread use in applications, such as web browsing, email, Internet faxing, instant messaging, and voice-over-IP ("VoIP").

C. Online Privacy Notices

Most organizations develop comprehensive privacy notices to communicate to the public the organization's information handling practices and policies. These privacy notices typically take the form of a detailed webpage accessible from the organization's homepage.

A privacy notice should include (1) a description of the types of information collected, (2) any uses or disclosures of the information, (3) choices available to the website user (e.g., opt-in or opt-out of certain activities), (4) contact information for the organization, and (5) the effective date of the notice. Privacy notices should also be regularly reviewed and any substantial changes communicated to the user. For example, when information is shared or used in a way not addressed by the privacy policy, users should be notified and the privacy notice updated to describe the new uses of the data.

The original goal of privacy notices was to create transparency in an organization's data collection practices and to help users make informed decisions. Unfortunately, most users do not read privacy notices because they are drafted in a verbose and legally formalistic manner. Layered privacy notices address this concern by presenting the user with a short notice that is simple and concise. This short notice summarizes the organization's information handling practices and the choices available to users. The full privacy notice is typically accessible by a hyperlink from the short notice if the user wants more information about the organization's privacy practices. Thus, layered notices provide a quick and easy way for a user to understand an organization's information handling practices and the choices available to the user.

D. Online Data Collection

Web forms are the most common mechanism for collecting personal information on the Internet. Web forms are a type of interface presented to a user of a website for inputting and transmitting data, including personal data. The three main input elements used by web forms to collect data are (1) text boxes, (2) checkboxes, and (3) radio buttons. From an information security perspective, check boxes and radio button are preferred because a user's input is limited. The user either checks the box or leaves it unchecked. Text boxes, on the other hand, allow a user to enter data that may cause unexpected results when processed by an application. For example, a user may enter a large amount of data into a text box which may cause a buffer overflow in a web application that tries to utilize the data. Therefore, text boxes should only be used when necessary and limits should be place on the size of the text box (i.e., the number of characters allowed to be entered into the text box).

There are two primary ways that websites collect data from users: (1) active data collection, and (2) passive data collection. Active data collection occurs when a user deliberately enters information in a web form or otherwise actively provides the information. Passive data collection, on the other hand, occurs when data is indirectly collected without any overt user interaction and generally includes capturing user preferences and usage behavior, including location data from personal mobile devices. The most widely used example of passive collection is the placement of web cookies on a user's computer to capture Internet browsing history.

E. Intrusions to Online Privacy

With billions of users on the Internet, there are bound to be some users with less than altruistic motives. Internet users face a numbers of intrusions to their privacy, some of which are illegal and others that are just annoying. Some of the more problematic intrusions are (1) spam, (2) malware, and (3) phishing.

Spam refers to unsolicited commercial email. Spam is also sometimes referred to as "bulk" commercial email because a large number of recipients typically receive the message. Spam can clog a user's mailbox, making him less productive and frustrated. Spam also often contains inappropriate content, such as an offer for sale of illegal prescription drugs or pirated software. Recently, spam accounted for more than 70% of all electronic messages, with more than 40 billion spam message sent each day.

Another abusive practice on the Internet is the distribution of malware. Malware, short for malicious software, is a computer program used or designed by attackers to disrupt a computer's operation, gather sensitive information, or gain access to a private computer system. Malware is a general term used to describe a variety of forms of intrusive software. Malware includes computer viruses, worms, Trojan horses, rootkits, keyloggers, spyware, adware, and other malicious programs.

Finally, phishing is the act of acquiring information, such as usernames, passwords, and credit card details, by masquerading as a trustworthy entity in an electronic communication. Electronic messages purporting to be from IT administrators, banks, and government agencies are commonly used to lure the unsuspecting receivers of the fraudulent communication. Phishing emails may contain links to websites that are infected with malware. One type of phishing called "spear phishing" is a phishing attempt directed at a specific individual or company. With spear phishing, an attacker gathers personal information about their often high-profile target to increase the probability of a successful attack. For example, an attacker may send an email to the chief financial officer ("CFO") of a company pretending to be the company's chief executive officer ("CEO"). In the message, the attacker may request that the CFO provide internal financial data by return message. Because the attacker has personalized the communication, the chances of the CFO actually sending the requested data are increased. This is an example of spear phishing.

F. Online Behavioral Advertising

Online behavioral advertising (also known as targeted advertising) refers to a range of technologies and techniques used by online advertisers that allow them to increase the effectiveness of their advertising campaigns by capturing data generated by website visitors. For example, a commercial website may track a user's browsing history and automatically serve advertisements for products related to the content previously viewed by the user. When targeted advertising is done without the knowledge of the user, it may be a breach of browser security and potentially even illegal.

In 2010, the Federal Trade Commission proposed a new regulatory framework for consumer data privacy, including a proposal for a "Do Not Track" mechanism which would allow Internet users to opt-out of online behavioral advertising. The FTC stated, "[t]he most practical method of providing uniform choice for online behavioral advertising would likely involve placing a setting similar to a persistent cookie on a consumer's browser and conveying that setting to sites that the browser visits, to signal whether or not the consumer wants to be tracked or receive targeted advertisements."

Web cookies (also known as HTTP cookies or browser cookies) are frequently used for online behavioral advertising. A web cookie is a small piece of data sent from a website and stored in a user's web browser while the user is browsing that website. Every time the user loads the website, the browser sends the cookie back to the server to notify the website of the user's previous activity. Web cookies were designed to reliably retain state information (such as items in a shopping cart) or to record the user's browsing activity, including clicking particular buttons, logging in, or recording which pages were visited by the user.

Web cookies are classified as either first-party or third-party cookies. First-party cookies are cookies that belong to the same domain as the webpage that a user is currently viewing (as indicated in the browser's address bar). Third-party cookies, on the other hand, are cookies that belong to domains different from the one shown in the address bar. For example, if you are viewing the website http://www.amazon.com, first-party cookies are those cookies from amazon.com. Third-party cookies would be those cookies from all other domains, such as doubleclick.net. Web pages can feature content from third-party domains (such as banner advertisements), which opens up the potential for tracking the user's browsing history. Privacy setting options in most modern browsers allow the blocking of third-party tracking cookies.

Web cookies are further classified as either session or persistent cookies. A session cookie (also known as an in-memory cookie or transient cookie) exists in temporary memory only while the user is reading and navigating the website. Web browsers delete session cookies when the user closes the browser or restarts his computer. A persistent cookie is written to disk and stored until the expiration date contained in the cookie. For example, if a persistent cookie has its expiration date set to 1 year, then within the year, the data in the cookie would be sent back to the server every time the user visited the server. The cookie would automatically expire upon the 1 year expiration date and be deleted from the user's computer. A persistent cookie could be used to record a vital piece of information, such as a user's login credentials. For this reason, persistent cookies are also called "tracking cookies." Persistent cookies enable the "remember me" functionality found on most websites that automatically logs a user into the website.

In the EU, the E-Privacy Directive of 2009 (also known as the Cookie Directive) recognizes the importance and usefulness of cookies for the functioning of modern Internet but also warns of the danger that cookies may present to privacy. Specifically, the Directive requires that the user provide affirmative consent before a cookie is stored on the user's computer. Therefore, much of Europe has adopted an opt-in approach to persistent web cookies, requiring a user's informed consent before cookies can be stored on the user's machine.

G. Recent Developments in Online Privacy

The section addresses two recent issues related to online privacy: (1) cloud computing and (2) mobile computing privacy. Both topics are frequently tested on the Certification Foundation exam.

1. Cloud Computing

Cloud computing is a colloquial expression used to describe a variety of different types of computing concepts that involve a large number of computers connected through a real-time communication network (typically, the Internet). Cloud computing relies on sharing of resources to achieve coherence and economies of scale similar to a utility (such as the electricity grid) but over a network. The five main characteristics of cloud computing are (1) on-demand capabilities, (2) broad network access, (3) resource pooling, (4) rapid elasticity, and (5) measured service.

There are three main service models of cloud computing: (1) Infrastructure as a Service ("IaaS"), (2) Platform as a Service ("PaaS"), and (3) Software as a service ("SaaS"). IaaS is the most basic cloud service model. In IaaS, users rent computing resources, such as storage, network capacity, and processing power from a cloud provider. The cloud provider owns the equipment and is responsible for housing, running, and maintaining it. Under PaaS, a cloud provider delivers a computing platform, typically including an operating system, database, and web server. Web developers build and publish web applications using the platform. Finally, SaaS is a software delivery model in which applications and associated data are centrally hosted in the cloud. Customers typically access the applications through a web browser over the Internet. SaaS is often referred to as "on-demand software."

Cloud computing may also be classified according to its deployment model. Four main types of clouds exist: (1) private clouds, (2) public clouds, (3) community clouds, and (4) hybrid clouds. A private cloud is operated solely for a single organization, whether managed or hosted internally or externally. A public cloud is offered to the general public through the Internet. Thus, public clouds are generally less secure than private clouds. Community clouds are collaborative efforts in which infrastructure is shared between several organizations from a specific community. For example, several auction websites may decide to join a community cloud for hosting their similar sites. Finally, a hybrid cloud is a composition of at least one private cloud and at least one public cloud. A hybrid cloud is typically offered in one of two ways: a vendor has a private cloud and forms a partnership with a public cloud provider, or a public cloud provider forms a partnership with a vendor that provides private cloud platforms.

2. Mobile Computing Privacy

Mobile computing devices are everywhere today. Most individuals in industrialized countries either carry a mobile computing device (e.g., a smart phone, laptop, or tablet) or may be readily associated with a mobile computing device, such as an automobile's entertainment and navigational hub that is connected to the Internet. The ubiquity of mobile computing devices has created new concerns for privacy practitioners. Chief among them is how mobile devices store, distribute, and secure location data.

Mobile devices today can determine and distribute a user's location using the global positioning system ("GPS") and other techniques in real-time. Consequently, location has become a new data element that has both privacy and security implications. Advertisers can target users based on their location (e.g., send an advertisement for a cold beverage in areas where the temperature is hot), criminals could target unsuspecting visitors to new cities, and the government could use location information to track an individual's movements. All of these situations highlight why location data is an often debated subject for privacy practitioners. When dealing with mobile computing devices, it is important to acknowledge and address the privacy issues associated with location information.

Chapter 4: Information Security

This chapter addresses procedures and techniques for securing information, in both electronic and paper form. You should expect anywhere from 12 to 14 questions on your examination directed to subject matter from this chapter.

A. Glossary Terms

Many questions on the exam come from definitions provided in the IAPP's glossary. Therefore, it is important that you read the definitions provided in the glossary for the terms listed below. The glossary is located at:

http://www.cippexam.com/glossary

Glossary Terms: Application-Layer Attacks, Authentication, Authorization, Biometrics, Breach Disclosure, Cloud Computing, Computer Forensics, Confidentiality, Cryptography, Data Breach, Encryption, Extranet, Information Privacy, Information Security, Internet Protocol Address, Internet Service Provider, Intrusion Detection System, Intrusion Prevention System, ISO 27002, Least Privilege, Local Area Network, Logs, Multi-factor Authentication, Network-Layer Attacks, Non-repudiation, Perimeter Controls, Privacy by Design, Public-key Infrastructure, Risk Assessment Factors, Role-based Access Controls, Secret Key, Trojan Horse, Virtual Private Network, Voice Over Internet Protocol, Wide Area Network.

B. Overview of Information Security Fundamentals

Information security is the practice of protecting information from unauthorized access, use, disclosure, disruption, or modification. The most well-known model for information security is called the C-I-A triad, referring to Confidentiality, Integrity, and Availability.

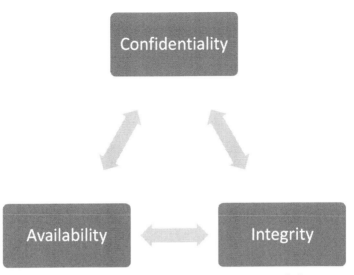

Figure 5: Information Security Model

The C-I-A model is a global framework and is reflected in numerous information privacy laws across the world. For example, in accordance with the 2009 Madrid Resolution, a data controller must protect personal data with appropriate safeguards to ensure its "integrity, confidentiality and availability."

With respect to the C-I-A model, confidentiality refers to preventing disclosure of information to unauthorized individuals or systems. Integrity refers to maintaining and assuring the accuracy and consistency of information over its entire lifecycle. Finally, availability refers to the ability of authorized users to access information.

Organizations implement information security by creating one or more controls or safeguards that mitigate the risk to the information. As previously addressed in Chapter 1, these controls are generally classified into three groups: (1) administrative, (2) physical, and (3) technical.

C. Information Security Policies

An information security policy is an internal statement that an organization adopts to describe the procedures in place that protect its informational assets. An information security policy should address the restrictions placed on an information technology system, such as password polices and access control mechanisms, and the users of the system, who may be employees of the organizations or outside vendors assisting the organization.

The International Organization for Standardization ("ISO") has developed standards related to information security. For example, ISO 27001 specifies a management system that is intended to bring information security under explicit management control. ISO 27001 requires that management (1) systematically examine the organization's information security risks, (2) design and implement a coherent and comprehensive suite of information security controls to address risks that are deemed unacceptable, and (3) adopt an overarching management process to ensure that the information security controls meet the organization's information security needs on an ongoing basis.

ISO 27002 is an information security standard that provides best practices for information security management. The standard defines information security within the context of the C-I-A triad: "the preservation of confidentiality (ensuring that information is accessible only to those authorized to have access), integrity (safeguarding the accuracy and completeness of information and processing methods), and availability (ensuring that authorized users have access to information and associated assets when required)." Organizations can use ISO 27001 and 27002 as the framework for an effective information security program.

D. Information Classification

When creating an information security policy, it is important to recognize that not all information should be treated equally. Confidential and sensitive information demands greater protection. Conversely, publicly available and well-known information typically requires less protection. An organization's information should be classified into several groups (depending upon its importance and sensitivity), and the appropriate controls should be placed around access to the groups of information.

The most common information classification scheme divides

information into three categories:

1. Public: information by its very nature is designed to be shared broadly, without restriction. Examples include marketing material, press releases, and regulatory reports submitted to government agencies.

2. Sensitive: information that is considered internal and should not be released outside of the organization. Examples include business plans, financial data, and documents reflecting corporate strategy.

3. Confidential: information that is generally intended for a very specific purpose and should not be disclosed to anyone without a demonstrated need to know. Examples include employee bank account information, social security numbers, and login credentials (e.g., username and password).

Typically, very few controls should be placed on public information. Controls suitable for public information include mechanisms that prevent unauthorized modification or alteration. For example, although a corporate press release is generally public information, an organization should prevent unauthorized individuals from altering the press release and thereby potentially disseminating incorrect or fraudulent information. Access to public information is generally not restricted.

For sensitive information, controls should prevent unauthorized modification or alteration and control access to the sensitive information. For example, sensitive information may be encrypted or password protected. In additional, logs may record who accesses or modifies sensitive information.

With respect to confidential information, additional controls should be implemented above and beyond the controls already in place for sensitive information. These include having individuals with access to the confidential information execute non-disclosure agreements and storing confidential information on a separate and secure data server.

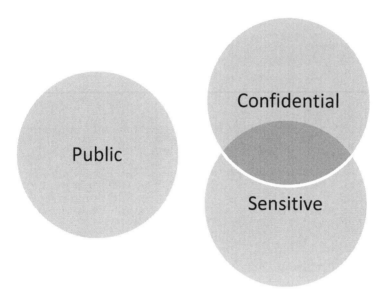

Figure 6: Standard Information Classifications

As shown in Figure 6, certain types of information may be both confidential and sensitive. Public information, however, generally cannot be confidential or sensitive because public information by its nature is already widely known.

E. Information Risk Assessment

Risk can be broadly defined as the likelihood of an undesirable event occurring after taking into account any controls in place to mitigate the undesirable event. An industry accepted formulation of information technology risk is:

$$Risk = \sum_{i=1}^{n} Threat_i * Vulnerability_i * Expected\ Loss_i$$

As indicated by the above formula, the total risk associated with an organization's information technology is directly related to three parameters: (1) threats, (2) vulnerabilities, and (3) expected loss. Threats are any circumstances that may cause an undesirable event, such as a data breach. Vulnerabilities are weaknesses in an organization's information systems, policies, or procedures. When a threat exploits some vulnerability, a security event that creates risk occurs. The amount of the risk for a particular security event is equal to the probability of the event occurring times the expected loss associated with the event. Summing the risk associated with all security events at an organization results in the total information risk.

The Certification Foundation exam typically contains several questions related to the formulation of risk. Therefore, you should know the basic formula and the three components used to calculate risk.

F. Technical Controls for Information Security

Technical controls are safeguards or countermeasures that help an organization avoid, counteract, or minimize security risks relating to information stored in an information technology system. Remember, these technical controls are just one of the three main type of information controls (the other two being administrative and physical controls).

Technical security controls can be classified into three primary types:

1. Preventive: controls designed to protect information before a security event occurs. Examples include firewalls, passwords, and encryption.

2. Detective: controls designed to protect information during a security event. Examples include security logs and intrusion detection systems.

3. Corrective: controls designed to protect information after a security event occurs. Examples include intrusion preventive systems that automatically block suspicious activity.

More than one type of control may be used to protect information. For example, confidential information should be protected by several controls of varying classes. Information of lower importance, such as public information, may be protected by fewer controls or even no controls.

Determining who at an organization has access to particular types of information is an important process that an organization must undertake when developing its security policy. As a general matter, employees should only be given access to information that is needed for them to fulfill their job responsibilities. No greater access should be provided. Role-based access controls are generally used to restrict system access to authorized roles and users at an organization.

G. Basic Principles of Information Security

When implementing security controls at an organization, it is important to keep in mind two basic tenets of information security. First is the principle of separation of duties. Separation of duties is the principle of requiring more than one person to complete a task. For example, before paying an invoice, an employee may need to submit an expense report. After submitting the expense report, it may be routed to a manager for approval before getting paid. By separating the ability to pay invoices into two requisite parts (i.e., expense report generation and approval), an organization deters fraud and reduces errors.

The second basic principle of information security is called the rule of least privilege. In accordance with this rule, a user should only be provided the minimum access needed to accomplish a legitimate business task. The rule of least privilege limits the damage that can be caused by a rogue employee by limiting the level of access given to the employee. Role-based access controls are a common way to implement the rule of least privilege. With role-based access, all users are classified into one of several defined roles. For example, the system administrator may create a first role for employees who merely enter data into the system. A second role may be created for employees who audit or edit the data. Finally, a third role may be created for managers who approve the data. Various levels of access are assigned to each role depending on the functionality required to perform the responsibilities assigned to the role.

Some information technology departments grant more access than needed in order to minimize the number of support calls related to access requests. For example, a user may be given the rights to install new applications onto the user's computer system even though all applications needed for the user's job have already been preinstalled onto the system. Although this may be a convenient solution for the information technology department, it presents a major threat to the security of an organization's data assets. Information security should be a well-thought-out plan with various predefined roles determining the amount of access given to any particular user.

H. Incident Management and Response

Despite an organization's best efforts, security breaches will inevitably occur. When an incident occurs, an organization must know how to appropriately respond. The basic incident management and response process includes: (1) incident discovery, (2) containment and analysis, (3) notification, and (4) eradication and future prevention.

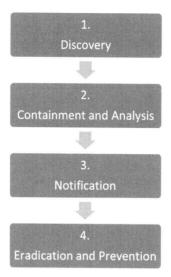

Figure 7: Incident Management Framework

The first step to incident management is discovery of the breach. After a breach is discovered, the breach should be contained by, for example, disabling affected user accounts. The containment process necessarily involves analysis of the breach to determine how it occurred. Notification is the third step when responding to a security breach. When and whom to notify will depend on an organization's information security and privacy policies, as well as any applicable laws and regulations. In some cases, no notification may be required (for example, when the breach was limited to just public, non-personal information). The final step is eradication and prevention. Once it is known how the incident occurred, appropriate remedial steps should be taken as soon as possible to prevent any future harm. Eradication involves the removal of the threat and vulnerability that enabled the breach, and prevention addresses the actions that will preclude a similar breach from occurring in the future.

The incident management process described above provides an organization with a framework for dealing with and responding to information security events. Various additional steps may be added depending upon then size of an organization and the regulatory environment that the organization operates within.

Conclusion

Congratulations! You have completed the text portion of this study guide. The information you have just read was designed to provide you with the fundamentals of information privacy and introduce you to the concepts that will be tested on the Certification Foundation exam. If you are new to information privacy, we recommend that you read the text a second time to ensure that you have fully absorbed and understand the material.

The next section of this guide contains sample questions with detailed answers. The questions are designed to supplement the material contained in the text portion of the guide. Therefore, do not worry if some of the concepts are new to you. The sample questions are designed to teach you new material and not to simply test your ability to remember the material presented in the beginning of this guide.

The questions below test facts that may appear on your exam. Thus, it is important that you carefully read both the questions and answers provided. You will likely receive dozens of questions on your examination that test similar facts as our sample questions. If you answer these questions correctly, you are well on your way to passing the Certification Foundation examination and becoming a certified privacy professional.

Sample Questions

1. Which of the following may be classified as an unfair trade practice by the FTC?

   A. A website's privacy notice clearly states that it will not encrypt sensitive personal information, and the website does not in fact encrypt the data

   B. An organization promises to honor opt-out requests within 10 days but fails to honor opt-out requests

   C. A rogue employee steals credit card information even though the organization took reasonable precautions to protect the credit card information

   D. A federally insured bank does not comply with a regulation prohibiting the bank from revealing information about its customers

ANSWER: A. Section 5 of the FTC Act prohibits "unfair or deceptive acts or practices in or affecting commerce." Answer A is an example of an unfair trade practice because the website is not being deceptive, but the potential harm caused by the website's failure to encrypt sensitive data clearly outweighs the cost of providing encryption, a commonplace and inexpensive security control. Answer B is an example of a deceptive trade practice. When companies tell consumers they will safeguard their personal information, the FTC can and does take law enforcement action to make sure that companies live up these promises. A violation of a promise made in a privacy notice is an example of a deceptive trade practice. Answer C would not be an unfair trade practice because the organization has implemented reasonable security measures, and the employee simply committed a crime, which is generally considered an unforeseeable event. Answer D is incorrect because the FTC has no jurisdiction over banks and common carriers, which are under the supervision of other governmental agencies.

2. In which service model of cloud computing are applications hosted by the cloud provider in the cloud and typically accessed by users through a web browser?

  A. Infrastructure as a service ("IaaS")
  B. Platform as a service ("PaaS")
  C. Software as a service ("SaaS")
  D. Network as a service ("NaaS")

ANSWER: C. With SaaS, applications are hosted by the cloud provider in the cloud. Customers typically access the applications through a web browser over the Internet. SaaS is often referred to as "on-demand software." IaaS is the most basic cloud service model. In IaaS, users rent computing resources, such as storage, network capacity, and processing power from cloud providers. The cloud provider owns the equipment and is responsible for housing, running, and maintaining it. Under PaaS, cloud providers deliver a computing platform, typically including an operating system, database, and web server. Web developers build and publish web applications using the platform.

3. Which of the following is NOT a principle set forth in the Guidelines on the Protection of Privacy and Transborder Flows of Personal Data adopted by the Organization for Economic Cooperation and Development in 1980 ("OECD Guidelines")?

  A. Collection Limitation
  B. Openness
  C. Mutual Consent
  D. Security Safeguards

ANSWER: C. The eight principles contained in the OECD guidelines are: (1) collection limitation principles, (2) data quality principle, (3) purpose specification principle, (4) use limitation principle, (5) security safeguards principle, (6) openness principle, (7) individual participation principle, and (8) accountability principle.

4. In which country is a person's tax return considered a public record?

   A. Canada
   B. Norway
   C. China
   D. Argentina

ANSWER: B. In Norway, tax returns are considered public records. Included within the tax return is a person's salary. Finland and Sweden also treat tax returns as public records.

5. Which country takes a co-regulatory approach to privacy protection?

   A. Israel
   B. Canada
   C. Zimbabwe
   D. Morocco

ANSWER: B. Canada, Australia, and New Zealand are three countries employing a co-regulatory model of privacy protection.

6. Which of the following is an industry standard formula for assessing information security risk?

   A. Risk = Threat x Vulnerability x Expected Loss
   B. Risk = Control - Threat / Vulnerability
   C. Risk = Threat + Vulnerability – Expected Loss
   D. Risk = Threat x Vulnerability / Control

ANSWER: A. As indicated by the correct formula, information security risk is directly related to three parameters: (1) threats, (2) vulnerabilities, and (3) expected loss. Threats are any circumstances that may cause an undesirable event, such as a data breach. Vulnerabilities are weaknesses in an organization's information systems, policies, or procedures. When a threat exploits some vulnerability, a security event that creates risk occurs. The amount of the risk for a particular security event is equal to the probability of the event occurring times the expected loss associated with the event. Answers B – D provide incorrect formulations of information security risk.

7. Information security policies and procedures should be communicated to which employees of an organization?

    A.   All employees
    B.   Employees in the information security department
    C.   Managers
    D.   The chief executive officer

ANSWER: A. All employees should be trained in information security best practices, and an organization's information security policies should be communicated to all employees, regardless of level. Even the lowest level employee can cause a security incident.

8. Which of the following is NOT generally performed by information security personnel at an organization?

    A.   Enforce compliance with the information security policy
    B.   Communicate information security policies to employees
    C.   Monitor for security incidents
    D.   Develop an overall corporate security strategy

ANSWER: D. While information security personnel can perform a wide range of tasks related to information security at an organization, generally an executive, such as the chief security officer, will develop the corporate security policy.

9. What is the name of the backward looking process used to analyze how effectively an information security program has operated in the past?

    A.   Monitoring
    B.   Observation
    C.   Assessment
    D.   Planning

ANSWER: C. An assessment is the process used to evaluate how an information security program has operated in the past. It generally includes an inventory all of data assets stored at an organization and the systems responsible for processing the data assets. Monitoring, observation, and planning are generally contemporaneous or forward looking processes.

10. Which one of the following is NOT a primary purpose of the APEC Privacy Framework, which was approved by the APEC ministers in 2004?

    A.   Improve information sharing among government agencies and regulators

    B.   Facilitate the safe transfer of information between economies

    C.   Encourage the use of electronic data as a means to enhance and expand business

    D.   Protect individuals from illegal data sharing practices

ANSWER: D. The Asia-Pacific Economic Cooperation ("APEC") Privacy Framework, which is consistent with the OECD's 1980 Guidelines, has the following primary goals: (1) improve information sharing among government agencies and regulators, (2) facilitate the safe transfer of information between economies, (3) establish a common set of privacy principles, (4) encourage the use of electronic data as a means to enhance and expand business, and (5) provide technical assistance to those economies that have yet to address privacy from a regulatory or policy perspective.

11. Which of the following is typically the final step when establishing an information security program?

    A.   Monitor and review compliance with the security program

    B.   Identify and evaluate risks

    C.   Define the security policy

    D.   Review complaints and evaluations

ANSWER: A. Generally, an information security program should be established by (1) defining the security policy and security management system; (2) identifying and evaluating any risks, (3) selecting appropriate controls to address the identified risks, (4) obtaining management approval of program, and (5) monitoring and reviewing compliance with the program.

12. Employee training on information security best practices is what type of security control?

A. Physical control
B. Administrative control
C. Technical control
D. Third-party control

ANSWER: B. Administrative controls are administrative actions, policies, and procedures that protect information. Employee training and incident response plans are types of administrative controls. Password authentication and firewalls are types of technical controls, while locks are physical controls.

13. Effective information security considers what three central factors?

A. Confidentiality, integrity, and availability
B. Accountability, integrity, and autonomy
C. Confidentiality, integrity, and autonomy
D. Redundancy, reliability, and availability

ANSWER: A. The most well-known model for information security is called the C–I–A triad, referring to Confidentiality, Integrity, and Availability. Confidentiality refers to preventing the disclosure of information to unauthorized individuals or systems. Integrity refers to maintaining and assuring the accuracy and consistency of information over its entire lifecycle. Lastly, availability refers to the ability of authorized users to access the information. The C–I–A model is a global framework and is reflected in numerous information privacy laws across the world.

14. The National Do Not Call Registry is primarily enforced by which entities?

    A.   Department of Transportation and FTC
    B.   U.S. Department of Justice and FTC
    C.   Department of Commerce and FCC
    D.   FTC and FCC

ANSWER: D. Pursuant to its authority under the Telephone Consumer Protection Act ("TCPA"), the Federal Communication Commission ("FCC") established, together with the Federal Trade Commission ("FTC"), a national Do Not Call Registry in 2003. The registry is nationwide in scope, applies to all telemarketers (with the exception of certain non-profit organizations), and covers both interstate and intrastate telemarketing calls. Commercial telemarketers are not allowed to call you if your number is on the registry, subject to certain exceptions. The FTC and FCC are the primary enforcers of the National Do Not Call Registry.

15. Which country released a report in February 2011 that provides guidance for utility companies on building smart grids with "privacy by design" principles?

    A.   United Stated
    B.   Canada
    C.   Germany
    D.   Australia

ANSWER: B. The Information and Privacy Commissioner of Ontario, Canada developed the "privacy by design" framework in the 1990s. It includes the following seven principles: (1) Proactive not Reactive; Preventative not Remedial; (2) Privacy as the Default Setting; (3) Privacy Embedded into Design, (4) Full Functionality — Positive-Sum, not Zero-Sum; (5) End-to-End Security — Full Lifecycle Protection; (6)Visibility and Transparency — Keep it Open; and (7) Respect for User Privacy — Keep it User-Centric. In February 2011, the Information and Privacy Commissioner released a report title "Operationalizing Privacy by Design: The Ontario Smart Grid Case Study." The report provides guidance for utility companies on building smart grids with privacy by design principles.

16. When do confidentiality and privacy issues exist with respect to human resources information?

   A. During candidate screening and through the interview process
   B. While the individual is a current employee of the organization
   C. After an employee is terminated by the organization
   D. All of the above

ANSWER: D. Confidentiality and privacy issues exist whenever an organization is holding personal information concerning its employees. Therefore, privacy issues exist as soon as personal information is communicated from the prospective candidate all the way up to and after termination.

17. Which of the following accurately describes the EU Data Protection Directive?

   A. It applies to personal information held by the private sector and not the government
   B. There are typically less strict legal rules for government organizations that hold personal information than for private organizations
   C. Sensitive information is referred to as "protected classes of data"
   D. Business contact information is classified as sensitive information

ANSWER: B. Although the EU Data Protection Directive applies to both the public and private sectors, generally less strict legal rules apply to government agencies than to private organizations. For example, processing of personal information can occur without consent if processing is necessary to perform tasks of public interest or tasks carried out by official authorities. The EU Data Protection Directive uses the term "special categories of data" to describe sensitive personal information (not "protected classes data"). In accordance with the Directive, special categories of data include personal data revealing racial or ethnic origin, political opinions, religious or philosophical beliefs, trade-union membership, and the processing of data concerning health or sex life. Business contact information is not classified as sensitive information.

18. Wiretaps laws are primary designed to protect what?

    A.   The identity of the sender and receiver of communications

    B.   The location of the sender and receiver of communications

    C.   The content of communications

    D.   The date and time of communications

ANSWER: C. Wiretapping is the monitoring of telephone and Internet conversations by a third party, often through covert means. Wiretap laws are primary designed to protect the content of communications, such as the content of a telephone call. While wiretaps can reveal the identity and location of the sender and receiver, as well as the date and time of a communication, these facts are all secondary types of information that may be protected by wiretap laws when disclosed by the content of the communication.

19. Which of the following is NOT a major reason why health information is considered sensitive in most jurisdictions?

    A.   Drug companies may market new and untested drugs to individuals with ailments if health information is not protected as sensitive information

    B.   Patients are forthcoming with their doctors when health information is protected as sensitive information

    C.   Employers may treat employees unequally and potentially discriminate against employees if health information was not classified as sensitive information

    D.   Health information relates to the inner workings of the individual's mind and body and therefore is inherently private

ANSWER: A. Answers B–D present the three major reasons why countries classify health information as sensitive information. The possibility of drug companies marketing new drugs to consumers is not a major reason why health information is classified as sensitive.

20. Which Middle East country requires that databases storing sensitive personal information be registered with the government?

    A.   Iran
    B.   Israel
    C.   Egypt
    D.   Jordan

ANSWER: B. Israel's Protection of Privacy law requires registration of any database that includes sensitive information. More specifically, it requires registration of a database if (1) the database includes information about more than 10,000 persons; (2) the database includes sensitive information; (3) the database includes information about persons and the information was not provided to the database by them, on their behalf or with their consent; (4) the database belongs to a public body; or (5) the database is used for direct mail.

21. Which Latin American country was one of the first countries to be deemed as providing as adequate level of protection by the EU Commission?

    A.   Argentina
    B.   Chile
    C.   Columbia
    D.   Uruguay

ANSWER: A. In 2003, Argentina became the first Latin American country to be deemed as providing as adequate level of protection by the EU Commission. Argentina was also the first Latin American country to enact an omnibus data protection and privacy law. Uruguay was deemed adequate in 2012. Chile and Columbia have not been deemed as providing an adequate level of protection.

22. Which types of records are covered by the federal Freedom of Information Act ("FOIA")?

    A.   Executive branch records
    B.   Congressional records
    C.   Judicial records
    D.   Records more than 10 years old

ANSWER: A. FOIA is a federal freedom of information law enacted in 1966 that allows for the full or partial disclosure of previously unreleased information and documents controlled by the United States government. FOIA explicitly applies only to executive branch government agencies and therefore does not include legislative and judicial branch records. FOIA defines agency records subject to disclosure, outlines mandatory disclosure procedures, and grants nine statutory exemptions to disclosure, such as records containing trade secrets.

23. When a website operator states in its privacy notice that it will not share financial information with third-parties and then shares financial information with a third-party affiliate, what recourse may occur?

    A.   The FTC may bring an action for unfair competition against the operator
    B.   The FTC may bring an action for deceptive trade practices against the operator
    C.   A user of the website may bring a criminal complaint against the operator
    D.   The FTC may bring an action under Section 7 of the FTC Act

ANSWER: B. If an organization fails to comply with its privacy notice, it may be held liable by the FTC for a deceptive trade practice under Section 5 of the FTC Act, which prohibits "unfair or deceptive acts or practices in or affecting commerce." When companies tell consumers they will safeguard their personal information, the FTC can and does take law enforcement action to make sure that companies live up to these promises. A violation of a promise made in a privacy notice is an example of a deceptive trade practice. The distinction between a deceptive trade practice and an unfair trade practice is often tested on the Certification Foundation exam.

24. The Children's Online Privacy Protection Act ("COPPA") applies to whom?

    A.   Operators of websites soliciting business in the United States

    B.   Operators of websites soliciting financial information from customers in the United States

    C.   Operators of commercial websites that are directed to children under 13 years of age

    D.   Operators of commercial websites that are directed to children under 18 years of age

ANSWER: C. COPPA was enacted in 1998 to curtail the collection of personal information from children. The Act applies to websites and online services operated for commercial purposes that are either directed to children under 13 or have actual knowledge that children under 13 are providing information online. In addition to requiring operators of these websites to conspicuously post a privacy notice, COPPA also requires that the website operator obtain verifiable parental consent prior to any collection, use, or disclosure of personal information from persons under age 13.

25. The Gramm–Leach–Bliley Act ("GLBA") applies to which organizations?

    A.   All organizations that process financial data

    B.   Financial organizations with more than 10,000 customers

    C.   All organizations regulated by the Department of Commerce

    D.   Domestic financial institutions

ANSWER: D. The GLBA, also known as the "Financial Services Modernization Act," was enacted in 1999. It applies to institutions that are significantly engaged in financial activities in the United States (also known as domestic financial institutions). The GLBA requires domestic financial institutions to, among other things, provide an initial privacy notice when the customer relationship is established and annually thereafter and provide an opt-out notice prior to sharing non-public personal information with non-affiliated third parties.

26. What is the main purpose of the Fair Credit Reporting Act ("FCRA")?

   A.   Enable data reporters to efficiently report valid debts on a consumer's credit report
   B.   Allow employers to quickly access financial data of their employees
   C.   Increase the ability of the government to access consumer reports of suspected criminals
   D.   Increase the accuracy and fairness of credit reporting and to limit the use of consumer reports to permissible purposes

ANSWER: D. The FRCA was originally enacted in 1970 and more recently was updated by the Fair and Accurate Credit Transactions Act of 2003 ("FACTA"). The FRCA applies to consumer reporting agencies ("CRAs"), such as Experian, TransUnion, and Equifax, and to users of consumer reports. The purpose of the FCRA was to increase the accuracy and fairness of credit reporting and to limit the use of consumer reports to permissible purposes, such as for employment and the underwriting of insurance.

27. What is the basic rule for processing protected health information under the Health Insurance Portability and Accountability Act ("HIPPA")?

A. Patients must opt-in before their protected health information is shared with other organizations unless the purpose is for treatment, payment, or healthcare operations

B. Patients must opt-out before their protected health information is shared with other organizations unless the purpose is for treatment, payment, or healthcare operations

C. Processing of protected health information is prohibited for all purposes without opt-in consent

D. Processing of protected health information is prohibited for all purposes without opt-out consent

ANSWER: A. Under HIPPA's Privacy Rule, covered entities may disclose protected heath information ("PHI") to facilitate treatment, payment, or health care operations without a patient's express written authorization. Any other disclosure of PHI requires the covered entity to obtain written authorization from the data subject for the disclosure (i.e., opt-in consent). In addition, when a covered entity discloses PHI, it also must make reasonable efforts to disclose only the minimum necessary information required to achieve its purpose.

28. In accordance with the Health Insurance Portability and Accountability Act ("HIPPA"), the Department of Health and Human Services ("HHS") has promulgated which of the following rules to address the handling of protected health information?

A. Transaction Rule and Equal Access Rule
B. Privacy Rule and the Security Rule
C. Privacy Rule and Equal Access Rule
D. Security Rule and the Notification Rule

ANSWER: B. The Health Insurance Portability and Accountability Act (HIPAA) was enacted in 1996 to define policies, procedures and guidelines that covered entities must adhere to for maintaining the privacy and security of individually identifiable protected health information ("PHI"). Covered entities generally include health care clearinghouses, employer sponsored health plans, health insurers, and health care providers. As directed by Title II of HIPPA, the Department of Health and Human Services ("HHS") has promulgated two important rules to address the handling of PHI: (1) the Privacy Rule and (2) the Security Rule.

29. Which of the following is NOT a privacy principle of the Safe Harbor program developed by the Department of Commerce in consultation with the European Commission?

A.   Notice
B.   Onward transfer to third parties
C.   Equal Opportunity
D.   Security

ANSWER: C. The European Union ("EU") Data Protection Directive prohibits the transfer of personal data to non-EU countries that do not meet the EU's "adequacy" standard for privacy protection. While the United States and the EU share the goal of enhancing privacy protection for their citizens, the United States takes a different approach to privacy from that taken by the EU. The U.S. Department of Commerce in consultation with the European Commission developed the Safe Harbor framework to bridge these differences in approach and provide a streamlined means for U.S. organizations to comply with the Directive. Organizations desiring to join the program must comply with the seven Safe Harbor privacy principles, which are: (1) notice, (2) choice, (3) onward transfer to third parties, (4) access, (5) security, (6) data integrity, and (7) enforcement.

30. A system log should record which events?

A.   Valid logins and invalid login attempts
B.   Database errors
C.   Application errors
D.   Device driver failure

ANSWER: D. A system log records events that are logged by the operating system and its components, such as device drivers. A security log is used to track security-related information on a computer system. The security log typically contains records of login/logout activity and other security-related events specified by the system's audit policy. An application log records events that are triggered by the applications used on a computer system, such as database applications. Events that are written to the application log are determined by the developers of the software program.

31. Which of the following accurately describes an organization's ability to monitor its employees in the EU?

    A.   Employee monitoring is permitted only within the physical areas owned by the organization

    B.   Employee monitoring is never permitted

    C.   Employee monitoring is permitted only with the express written consent of the employee

    D.   Employee monitoring is permitted only when necessary for a specific purpose

ANSWER: D. In Europe, once an employer decides to monitor an employee, the Article 29 Working Party suggests that the organization follow the following seven basic principles: (1) an employer must determine whether the monitoring is absolutely necessary for the specified purpose, (2) data collected through the monitoring must respond to a "specified, explicit and legitimate" purpose and cannot be processed for a different purpose, (3) the employer must provide clear and open notice to employees about the monitoring, (4) employers may monitor only to safeguard their legitimate interests, while not violating an employee's fundamental rights, (5) personal data processed in connection with the monitoring must be adequate, relevant, and not excessive, (6) personal data must be updated and retained only for the period deemed necessary for the purpose to be achieved, and (7) the employer must implement all appropriate technical and organizational measures to ensure that any personal data is protected from alteration, unauthorized access, and misuse.

32. Which of the following accurately describes the provisions of the EU e-Privacy Directive?

    A.   The Directive takes an opt-out approach to unsolicited commercial electronic communications

    B.   The Directive takes an opt-in approach to unsolicited commercial electronic communications

    C.   The Directive requires express written consent for marketing to minors

    D.   The Directive allows inferred consent for marketing to minors

ANSWER: B. The EU e-Privacy Directive takes an opt-in approach to unsolicited commercial electronic communications (that is, users must have given their prior consent before such communications are addressed to them). The Directive does not expressly address marketing to minors.

33. What is the effect of incorporating the standard contractual clauses of a model contract approved by the EU Commission into an international agreement between a data controller located in the Germany and a data processor incorporated in the United States?

    A.   Personal data may flow from the data processor to the data controller

    B.   Personal data may flow from the data controller to the data processor

    C.   The data controller is now a company providing an adequate level of protection

    D.   The data controller may now transfer personal data within the EU member states

ANSWER: B. After incorporating the standard contractual clauses of a model contract into an agreement, personal data may flow from a data controller established in any of the 27 EU member states and three EEA member countries (Norway, Liechtenstein and Iceland) to a data controller or to a data processor established in a country not ensuring an adequate level of data protection, such as the United States. The EU Commission has so far issued two sets of standard contractual clauses for transfers to data controllers established outside the EU/EEA and one set of contractual clauses to data processors established outside the EU/EEA. A is incorrect because model contracts affect the ability to transfer personal data out of the EU and into countries that do not provide an adequate level of protection. C is incorrect because as a data controller in Germany operating under German law the data controller is already operating in a country that provides an adequate level of protection. D is incorrect because the data controller is capable of transmitting personal data within the EU by virtue of being in compliance with German law and no model contract is needed. Again, model contracts permit the transfer of personal information outside the EU into countries not providing an adequate level of protection, such as the United States.

34. Which of the following is NOT an exception to the EU Data Protection Directive's requirement that transfers of personal data may only be made to countries which ensure an adequate level of protection?

A.   The transfer is necessary for the performance of a contract between the data subject and the controller
B.   The transfer is necessary in order to protect the vital interests of the data subject
C.   The transfer is necessary or legally required on important public interest grounds
D.   The transfer is made to the data subject's next of kin or guardian

ANSWER: D. Article 26(1) of the EU Data Protection Directive states that transfers of personal data to a country which do not ensure an adequate level of protection may take place if the data subject has "given his consent unambiguously to the proposed transfer." Other exceptions include: (1) the transfer is necessary for the performance of a contract between the data subject and the controller, (2) the transfer is necessary for the conclusion or performance of a contract concluded in the interest of the data subject, (3) the transfer is necessary or legally required on important public interest grounds, and (4) the transfer is necessary in order to protect the vital interests of the data subject. A – C set forth valid exceptions. Transfers to the data subject's next of kin or guardian are not exempted.

35. Which of the following is a major criticism of comprehensive privacy and data protection laws?

    A.   Cost of compliance outweighs the benefits in many industries
    B.   Incompatible with the regimes of other countries
    C.   Encourages innovation in data processing
    D.   Do not adequately protect personal information of minors

ANSWER: A. The main criticism of comprehensive privacy and data protection laws is that the cost of compliance outweighs the benefits in many industries. For example, onerous laws protecting sensitive information, such as health information, may be warranted in some cases, but the same level of protection may not be needed for less sensitive information in other industries. A second major criticism of comprehensive privacy and data protection laws is that they discourage innovation in data processing because regulatory approval is first needed before organizations may use personal information in potentially innovative ways (for example, with online social networking). These regulatory hurdles may discourage innovation.

36. Which of the following are the main reasons why countries adopt comprehensive privacy and data protection laws?

    A.   To secure international approval and combat online piracy
    B.   To combat online piracy and protect personal freedoms
    C.   To increase the costs of entering into a new market and remedy past injustices
    D.   To remedy past injustices and encourage electronic commerce

ANSWER: D. Remedying past injustices and encourage electronic commerce are two of the main reasons that countries enact comprehensive privacy and data protection laws. Countries also enact comprehensive privacy law to ensure consistency with other comprehensive regimes, such as the EU and its Data Protection Directive. Securing international approval, combating online piracy, protecting personal freedoms, and increasing the costs of entering into a new market are not the main reasons why countries adopt comprehensive privacy laws.

37. Which country has NOT joined the European Economic Area ("EEA") but is part of the European Free Trade Association ("EFTA")?

    A.   Switzerland
    B.   Norway
    C.   Liechtenstein
    D.   Iceland

ANSWER: A. Switzerland rejected the EEA agreement in a national referendum on December 6, 1992. It is, however, along with Norway, Liechtenstein, and Iceland, a current member of EFTA.

38. Which of the following may be considered personal information?

    A.   Information about an organization's competitors
    B.   Information about a company's financial well being
    C.   Information about an organization's business leads or prospects
    D.   Information about a company's physical address

ANSWER: C. Personal information is any information about an identified or identifiable individual. An organization's customers and prospects may be individuals, and therefore information about them may be classified as personal information. The other answer choices all relate to information about an organization as opposed to an individual, and therefore are not types of personal information.

39. Which country's privacy laws set forth specific and detailed requirements for the data protection officer ("DPO") of an organization?

    A.   Germany
    B.   Canada
    C.   New Zealand
    D.   Australia

ANSWER: A. A data protection officer ("DPO") is an individual (or group of individuals) responsible for data protection and privacy issues at an organization. Many organizations in Germany are obligated to formally appoint a data protection officer. Generally, companies that permanently employ ten or more persons in the automated processing of personal data are required to appoint a DPO. Each DPO must have intimate knowledge of Germany's data protection laws and possess other defined skills. Noncompliance may results in administrative fines for the organization. Most countries other than Germany do not have specific requirements for the DPO.

40. What was one of the primary purposes of the 2009 Madrid Resolution regarding the International Standards on the Protection of Personal Data and Privacy?

    A.   To protect minors from the unauthorized collection of personal information

    B.   To define a set of principles and rights guaranteeing the effective and internationally uniform protection of privacy

    C.   To establish penalties for those responsible for violating the privacy rights of individuals

    D.   To limit the use of automated processing of personal data

ANSWER: B. The stated purposes of the International Standards on the Protection of Personal Data and Privacy, which was adopted as part of the 2009 Madrid Resolution, are to (1) define a set of principles and rights guaranteeing the effective and internationally uniform protection of privacy with regards to the processing of personal data and (2) facilitate the international flow of personal data needed in a globalized world.

41. Which of the following is NOT a principle of the Asia-Pacific Economic Cooperation ("APEC") Privacy Framework adopted in 2004?

    A.   Preventing harm
    B.   Notice
    C.   Active enforcement
    D.   Collection limitation

ANSWER: D. The Asia-Pacific Economic Cooperation ("APEC") Privacy Framework, which is consistent with the OECD's 1980 Guidelines, has the following principles: (1) preventing harm, (2) notice, (3) collection limitation, (4) uses of personal information, (5) choice, (6) integrity of personal information, (7) security safeguards, (8) access and correction, and (9) accountability.

42. Which of the following accurately describes the use of public-key cryptography?

    A.   Sender uses recipient's public key to encrypt and receiver uses his public key to decrypt
    B.   Sender uses sender's private key to encrypt and receiver uses sender's public key to decrypt
    C.   Sender uses recipient's private key to encrypt and receiver uses his public key to decrypt
    D.   Sender uses recipient's public key to encrypt and receiver uses his private key to decrypt

ANSWER: D. Public-key cryptography (also called asymmetric-key cryptography) uses a pair of keys to encrypt and decrypt content. Each user has a pair of cryptographic keys – a public encryption key and a private decryption key. The public key is widely distributed, while the private key is known only to its owner. The keys are related mathematically, but the parameters used to generate the keys are chosen so that calculating the private key from the public key is virtually impossible.

43. What type of log should record events related to a database?

    A.   Security log
    B.   System log
    C.   Application log
    D.   Device log

ANSWER: C. An application log records events that are triggered by the applications used on a computer system, such as a database application. Events that are written to the application log are determined by the developers of the software program, not the operating system. A security log is used to track security-related information on a computer system. The log typically contains records of login/logout activity and other security-related events specified by the system's audit policy. A system log contains events that are logged by the operating system and its components, such as device drivers.

44. Which type of security measure may be used to prevent a cookie poisoning attack?

    A.   Encryption
    B.   Firewall
    C.   Intrusion detection system
    D.   Antivirus software

ANSWER: A. Cookie poisoning is the modification of a web cookie by an attacker in hopes of gaining unauthorized information about the user for purposes such as identity theft. To guard against cookie poisoning, websites that use them should protect cookies (through encryption, for example) before they are sent to a user's computer.

45. Which country has been deemed as providing an adequate level of privacy protection by the EU Commission?

    A.   Israel
    B.   Australia
    C.   Argentina
    D.   Morocco

ANSWER: C. Major countries that have been deemed adequate by the European Commission are Switzerland, Canada, Andorra, Argentina, Iceland, Liechtenstein, and Israel.

46. This country takes a co-regulatory approach to privacy?

    A.   Germany
    B.   Australia
    C.   Zimbabwe
    D.   Morocco

ANSWER: B. Canada, Australia, and New Zealand are three major countries employing a co-regulatory model of privacy protection.

47. Which of the following is NOT a requirement of the Personal Information Protection and Electronic Documents Act ("PIPEDA")?

    A.   Organizations covered by the Act must obtain an individual's consent when they collect, use or disclose the individual's personal information
    B.   The individual has a right to access personal information held by an organization and to challenge its accuracy, if need be
    C.   Personal information can only be used for the purposes for which it was collected
    D.   Organizations covered by the Act must provide annual privacy notice to their customers

ANSWER: D. PIPEDA is a Canadian data privacy law that codifies the fair information principles. Therefore, A—C are requirements of the Act. Annual privacy notices are not required as long as an organization's rules for processing personal information are clear and transparent.

48. Which of the following statements accurately describes the information quality principle?

    A.   Information should only be accessible to those with a need to know

    B.   Information should be accurate, complete, and relevant to the purposes of processing

    C.   Sensitive information should be protected with greater security than non-sensitive information

    D.   Information should be destroyed when it is no longer needed

ANSWER: B. Information quality is evaluated according to three metrics: (1) accuracy, (2) completeness, and (3) relevancy. Although the other answers all convey general information security principles, only answer B is directly related to information quality.

49. Which of the following is NOT a principle of privacy by design?

    A.   Opt-in choice

    B.   Privacy as the default setting

    C.   Proactive not reactive

    D.   End to end security

ANSWER: A. The Information and Privacy Commissioner of Ontario, Canada developed the privacy by design framework in the 1990s. It includes the following seven principles: (1) Proactive not Reactive; Preventative not Remedial; (2) Privacy as the Default Setting; (3) Privacy Embedded into Design, (4) Full Functionality — Positive-Sum, not Zero-Sum; (5) End-to-End Security — Full Lifecycle Protection; (6)Visibility and Transparency — Keep it Open; and (7) Respect for User Privacy — Keep it User-Centric. Opt-in choice is not a principle of privacy by design.

50. Which of the following is NOT a main reason for organizations to protect personal information?

    A.   Prevention of data breaches
    B.   Compliance with regulations
    C.   Increased cost
    D.   Avoidance of lawsuits

ANSWER: C. Increased cost is not a reason for organizations to protect personal information. Prevention of data breaches, compliance with law and regulation, and avoidance of lawsuits and regulatory actions are the main drivers for protecting personal information. Additional drivers include customer expectations and reputation.

51. Article 8 of the European Convention on Human Rights ("ECHR") provides protection for what privacy right?

    A.   Electronic communications
    B.   DNA profile
    C.   IP address
    D.   Private and family life

ANSWER: D. Article 8 of the ECHR provides a right to respect for one's "private and family life, his home and his correspondence," subject to certain restrictions.

52. Falsifying or "spoofing" a network address, so that information is sent to an attacker as opposed to its intended recipient, is what type of attack?

    A.   Robust attack
    B.   Redundant attack
    C.   Network layer attack
    D.   Application layer attack

ANSWER: C. Network layer attacks are those that exploit the networking protocol. Spoofing and denial of service ("DoS") attacks are two types of network layer attacks. Application layer attacks exploit applications running on network servers, such as email and database applications. Application layer attacks are the most common type of attacks because any given network may have dozens of network applications that may be exploited.

53. Which security mechanism is used for preventing unauthorized access to internal networks?

  A.   Firewall
  B.   Encryption
  C.   Intrusion detection system
  D.   Antivirus software

ANSWER: A. Firewalls are software or hardware solutions that prevent certain types of network traffic from entering an internal network in accordance with the firewall's policy. The other types of security mechanisms provided do not prevent unauthorized access to internal networks.

54. Which of following organizations does NOT provide industry standard best practices for information security?

  A.   International Organization for Standardization ("ISO")
  B.   National Institute of Standards in Technology ("NIST")
  C.   IT Governance Institute
  D.   Association of Computer Engineers and Technician ("ACET")

ANSWER: D. ISO, NIST, and the IT Governance Institute are all organizations that provide standards for information security best practices.

55. What is the most common form of monitoring employed in an information security system?

  A.   Intrusion detection systems
  B.   System logs
  C.   Key loggers
  D.   Video monitoring

ANSWER: B. System logs that record security related events, such as valid and invalid logins, are the most common form of monitoring in an information security system.

56. What is the initial step when creating an effective information security system for an existing organization?

    A.   Define the security policy
    B.   Select controls for managing risk
    C.   Identify, analyze, and evaluate risk
    D.   Conduct an information assessment

ANSWER: D. An information assessment is the first step when creating an effective information security system. Before a privacy practitioner can develop an information security system, he must assess what information is currently being collected at the organization and what information technology systems are being used to process the information. Only after the practitioner has a solid understanding of the information and systems in place can he develop an effective information security system.

57. What step should be performed first after defining the security policy when creating an information security program?

    A.   Monitor and periodically review the security program
    B.   Select controls for managing risk
    C.   Identify, analyze, and evaluate risk
    D.   Establish the scope of the information security system

ANSWER: C. The basic procedure for creating an information security program is (1) establish the scope of the information security system, (2) define the security policy, (3) establish a protocol for risk assessment, (4) identify, analyze, and evaluate risk, (5) select controls for managing the identified risk, (6) obtain management approval of any residual risk, and (7) monitor and periodically review the security program.

58. Which of the following is NOT a main source of information security requirements?

A.   Customer complaints and recommendations
B.   Threats and vulnerabilities of an organization
C.   Legal, regulatory, and contractual obligations
D.   An organization's information security and privacy policies

ANSWER: A. Customer complaints and recommendations are not a source of security requirements. Generally, an organization should have reasonable security protecting personal information based on the C-I-A triad. To provide reasonable security, threats and vulnerabilities of an organization must be analyzed to determine the level of risk. Laws, regulations, and contracts that an organization has entered into generally contain security requirements for an organization. An organization's information security and privacy policies generally include security requirements for different classes of information held or collected by the organization.

59. What is the relationship between information security and information privacy?

A.   Information security is concerned only with the unauthorized access of personal information, whereas information privacy addresses the use and confidentiality of personal information
B.   Information security is a necessary component of information privacy
C.   Information privacy is a subset of information security
D.   Information security is concerned with the unauthorized access, use, and confidentiality of personal information, whereas information privacy addresses only the use of personal information

ANSWER: B. Both information security and information privacy deal with the access, use, and confidentiality of information. Information security is one necessary component of information privacy. Information privacy also addresses the data subject's rights with respect to the personal information (i.e., the right to correct and control processing of his personal information).

60. In which cloud computer service model do users rent computing resources, such as storage, network capacity, and other resources?

    A.   Software as a service (SaaS)
    B.   Platform as a service (PaaS)
    C.   Infrastructure as a service (IaaS)
    D.   Hardware as a service (HaaS)

ANSWER: C. IaaS is the most basic cloud service model. In IaaS, users rent computing resources, such as storage, network capacity, and processing power from cloud providers. The cloud provider owns the equipment and is responsible for housing, running, and maintaining it. Under PaaS, cloud providers deliver a computing platform, typically including an operating system, database, and web server. Web developers build and publish web applications using the platform. Finally, with SaaS, applications are hosted by the cloud vendor in the cloud. Customers typically access the applications through a web browser over the Internet. SaaS is often referred to as "on-demand software."

61. Which organization is developing standards for Do Not Track approach to online targeted advertising?

    A.   International Organization for Standardization ("ISO")
    B.   Federal Trade Commission ("FTC")
    C.   World Wide Web Consortium ("W3C")
    D.   National Institute of Standards and Technology ("NIST")

ANSWER: C. The Tracking Protection Working Group of the W3C is developing standards for online targeted advertising, including Do Not Track specifications.

62. The EU e-Privacy Directive requires what type of consent before a cookie may be placed on a user's computer?

   A.   Written consent
   B.   Affirmative consent
   C.   Opt-out consent
   D.   Parental consent

ANSWER: B. The EU e-Privacy Directive requires affirmative, opt-in consent for cookies. Specifically, the Directive requires that "the subscriber or user concerned has given his or her consent, having been provided with clear and comprehensive information."

63. The National Advertising Initiative ("NAI") manages a self-regulatory pledge related to which of the following?

   A.   Direct mail marketing
   B.   Commercial email advertising
   C.   Sponsored search results
   D.   Online targeted advertising

ANSWER: D. The NAI's Code of Conduct is a set of self-regulatory principles that require NAI member companies to provide notice and choice with respect to Interest-based advertising and specifically online targeted advertising. Advertising networks which satisfy the NAI principles must provide consumers a choice about whether information collected about them is tracked and used to provide targeted advertising.

64. The Do Not Call Registry applies to what type of marketing?

   A.   Email marketing
   B.   Telemarketing
   C.   Unsolicited commercial messages
   D.   Educational marketing

ANSWER: B. Pursuant to its authority under the Telephone Consumer Protection Act ("TCPA"), the Federal Communication Commission ("FCC") established, together with the Federal Trade Commission ("FTC"), a national Do Not Call Registry in 2003. The registry is nationwide in scope, applies to all telemarketers (with the exception of certain non-profit organizations), and covers both interstate and intrastate telemarketing calls. Commercial telemarketers are not allowed to call you if your number is on the registry, subject to certain exceptions.

65. Which of the following statements concerning PIPEDA is false?

    A.   PIPEDA applies to only private organizations
    B.   Under PIPEDA, an organization may disclose personal information without the consent of the data subject for debt collection purposes
    C.   The Commissioner may audit any organization collecting personal information on Canadian citizens
    D.   An organization may use personal information without consent of the data subject in emergency situations

ANSWER: A. PIPEDA applies to every organization across Canada that collects, uses or discloses personal information in the course of commercial activities.

66. Data protection laws in Latin American are largely based on what principle?

    A.   Ombudsmen
    B.   Sensitive categories of data
    C.   Habeas data
    D.   Data protection authorities

ANSWER: C. Habeas data is a writ and constitutional remedy available in most Latin American countries. The literal translation from Latin of habeas data is "you have the data." The remedy varies from country to country, but in general, it is designed to protect, by means of an individual complaint presented to a constitutional court, the image, privacy, honor, and freedom of information of a person.

67. Which of the following is false regarding European privacy laws?

A.   European law is based on the tenant that privacy is a fundamental right
B.   The EU Data Protection Directive authorizes transfer of personal data to countries outside the EU if the country provides an adequate level of protection
C.   The EU Data Protection Directive applies to all sectors of industry and all types of personal information
D.   The EU Data Protection Directive substantially increased Switzerland's controls over financial data

ANSWER: D. The EU Data Protection Directive applies to countries of the European Economic Area ("EEA"), which includes all EU countries, and in addition, non-EU countries Iceland, Liechtenstein, and Norway. Switzerland rejected the EEA agreement and therefore is not bound by the EU Data Protection Directive. Switzerland has, however, passed a comprehensive data privacy that has been deemed adequate by the European Commission.

68. Which state was the first to enact rules governing the use and disclosure of consumer energy information from smart grids in the United States?

A.   California
B.   Florida
C.   Connecticut
D.   Massachusetts

ANSWER: A. The smart grid is an advanced metering system made up of smart meters capable of recording detailed and real time data on consumer electricity usage that is then sent to a central hub for processing. In 2011, the California Public Utilities Commission ("CPUC") established privacy rules for California's Smart Grid that covered the collection of customer usage data from the electricity grid.

69. In which country is a person's salary considered a public record?

   A.   Canada
   B.   Sweden
   C.   China
   D.   Argentina

ANSWER: B. In Sweden, tax returns are considered public records. Included within the tax return is a person's salary. Finland and Norway also treat tax returns as public records.

70. Which data element has recently become important because of the increasing use of smart phones?

   A.   Voice recordings
   B.   Telephone records
   C.   IP address
   D.   Location

ANSWER: D. Location is a data element that is becoming increasingly important from a privacy perspective. Smart phones and other telecommunications devices can determine your precise location and relay your location in real-time to a central server, which could then be accessed by the government or others.

71. What is the original purpose of bank secrecy laws?

   A.   To enable banks to better share information
   B.   To protect customer's financial information
   C.   To permit access of financial data by government authority for national security purposes
   D.   To ensure creditors have appropriate access to a debtor's financial information

ANSWER: B. Bank secrecy is a legal principle in some jurisdictions under which banks are not allowed to provide to authorities personal and account information about their customers unless certain conditions apply (for example, a criminal complaint has been filed). Bank secrecy laws are routinely criticized because they may enable money laundering.

72. Which of the following is correct regarding the Gramm–Leach–Bliley Act of 1999 ("GLBA")?

    A.   The Act is based on the permissible purpose approach to privacy
    B.   The Act covers all financial information, including publicly available information
    C.   The Act requires opt-in consent when sharing financial information with unaffiliated third-parties
    D.   The Act established a complicated set of privacy and security requirements for all financial institutions

ANSWER: D. GLBA is based on the fair information practices approach to privacy and not the permissible use approach. GLBA also does not cover publicly available information, and the sharing of financial data with unaffiliated third parties is permitted with opt-out consent.

73. This country takes a co-regulatory approach to privacy protection similar to that of Australia?

    A.   Israel
    B.   New Zealand
    C.   Zimbabwe
    D.   Morocco

ANSWER: B. Canada, Australia, and New Zealand are three countries employing a co-regulatory model of privacy protection.

74. After the Article 29 Working Party favorably evaluated this county's privacy law in 2010, the European Commission formally approved this country as providing adequate protection in 2012?

    A.   Uruguay
    B.   Mexico
    C.   Hong Kong
    D.   Japan

ANSWER: A. Uruguay was deemed adequate in 2012. Before Uruguay, the Working Party favorably evaluated Israel in 2009 and the European Commission formally approved Israel as providing adequate protection in 2011.

75. Japan's Act on the Protection of Personal Information Act defines "principal" as what entity?

    A.   Data processor
    B.   Data controller
    C.   Data subject
    D.   Data importer

ANSWER: C. In accordance with Japan's Protection of Personal Information Act, the term "principal" or "person" is the specific individual identified by the personal information (that is, the data subject).

76. Which Middle East country requires that databases of more than 10,000 persons be registered with the government?

    A.   Iran
    B.   Israel
    C.   Egypt
    D.   Iraq

ANSWER: B. Israel's Protection of Privacy law requires registration of any database that includes information about more than 10,000 persons. More specifically, it requires registration of a database if (1) the database includes information about more than 10,000 persons; (2) the database includes sensitive information; (3) the database includes information about persons and the information was not provided to the database by them, on their behalf or with their consent; (4) the database belongs to a public body; or (5) the database is used for direct mail. In 2011, the EU Commission decided that Israel is a country providing an adequate level of protection.

77. Which of the following is NOT exempt from disclosure under the Freedom of Information Act ("FOIA")?

A. Records containing trade secrets
B. Records containing the location of oil wells
C. Records describing the data handling practices of financial institutions
D. Records pertaining to federal regulatory agencies, federal employees, and federal agents

ANSWER: D. FOIA has the following nine exemptions: (1) those documents properly classified as secret in the interest of national defense or foreign policy; (2) related solely to internal personnel rules and practices; (3) specifically exempted by other statutes; (4) a trade secret or privileged or confidential commercial or financial information obtained from a person; (5) a privileged inter-agency or intra-agency memorandum or letter; (6) a personnel, medical, or similar file the release of which would constitute a clearly unwarranted invasion of personal privacy; (7) compiled for law enforcement purposes; (8) contained in or related to examination, operating, or condition reports about financial institutions; and (9) those documents containing exempt information about gas or oil wells. Answers A, B, and C fall in exemptions (4), (9), and (8), respectively. Answer D is not a recognized exemption and therefore is the correct answer.

78. The Children's Online Privacy Protection Act ("COPPA") prevents website operators from performing what activity?

A. Creating a website with content designed for children under 13 years of age
B. Collecting personal information from children under 13 years of age
C. Displaying a picture of a child after obtaining verifiable parental consent
D. Operating a website that is geared towards children in the United States with storage servers located outside the United States

ANSWER: B. Generally, COPPA applies to the online collection of personal information from children under 13 years of age. COPPA details what a website operator must include in a privacy policy, when and how to seek verifiable consent from a parent or guardian, and what responsibilities an operator has to protect children's privacy and safety online including restrictions on the marketing to those under 13.

79. Which is the most appropriate mechanism for enabling a multinational European corporation to transfer data concerning EU residents from Europe to an office in the United States?

    A.   Binding corporate rules
    B.   Contractual assurances
    C.   U.S. Safe Harbor program
    D.   Implicit consent

ANSWER: A. Binding corporate rules ("BCR") are internal rules adopted by a multinational group of related companies which define its global policy with regard to the international transfers of personal data within the same corporate group to entities located in countries which do not provide an adequate level of protection. Because the EU Commission has not deemed the U.S. as providing an adequate level of protection, a multinational corporation in Europe may adopt binding corporate rules with its offices in the U.S. to comply with the EU Data Protection Directive.

80. What is one of the purposes of the FCRA?

    A.   Give employers the right to correct credit reports for their employees
    B.   Encourage the dissemination of consumer data to foreign companies with a need to know the data
    C.   Limit the use of consumer reports to permissible purposes
    D.   Allow data reporters to place a debt on a consumer's credit report if they have a reasonable suspicion of the debt

ANSWER: C. Under the FCRA, a credit report (also called "consumer report") may only be acquired for a "permissible purpose." Section 604 of the FCRA sets forth the circumstances that are considered permissible, including with the written instructions of the consumer to whom the credit report relates. Thus a consumer's consent is a permissible purpose for obtaining a credit report under the FCRA.

81. When transferring personal data from Europe to the United States, which type of consent in needed from the data subjects?

    A.   Implied consent
    B.   Unambiguous consent
    C.   General consent
    D.   Advance consent

ANSWER: B. Article 26(1) of the EU Data Protection Directive states that transfers of personal data to a third countries which do not ensure an adequate level of protection may take place if the data subject has "given his consent unambiguously to the proposed transfer." Other exceptions include: (1) the transfer is necessary for the performance of a contract between the data subject and the controller, (2) the transfer is necessary for the conclusion or performance of a contract concluded in the interest of the data subject, (3) the transfer is necessary or legally required on important public interest grounds, and (4) the transfer is necessary in order to protect the vital interests of the data subject.

82. In accordance with the EU Data Protection Directive, unambiguous consent is achieved through what action?

    A.   An advanced waiver of right
    B.   An express verbal indication
    C.   Any freely given specific and informed indication
    D.   None of the above

ANSWER: C. In accordance with the EU Data Protection Directive, the data subject's unambiguous consent means "any freely given specific and informed indication of his wishes by which the data subject signifies his agreement to personal data relating to him being processed."

83. Which regulatory agencies do NOT enforce or certify compliance with the U.S. Safe Harbor program?

 A. FTC
 B. Department of Transportation
 C. FCC
 D. Department of Commerce

ANSWER: C. The European Union ("EU") Data Protection Directive prohibits the transfer of personal data to non-European Union countries that do not meet the European Union (EU) "adequacy" standard for privacy protection. While the United States and the EU share the goal of enhancing privacy protection for their citizens, the United States takes a different approach to privacy from that taken by the EU. The U.S. Department of Commerce in consultation with the European Commission developed the Safe Harbor framework to bridge these differences in approach and provide a streamlined means for U.S. organizations to comply with the Directive. Only U.S. organizations subject to the jurisdiction of the Federal Trade Commission ("FTC") or U.S. air carriers and ticket agents subject to the jurisdiction of the Department of Transportation ("DoT") may participate in the Safe Harbor program. The FTC and DoT enforce the program while the Department of Commerce receives annually certifications of compliance from those organizations participating in the program.

84. Which of the following is not considered an example of the self-regulatory model of data protection?

 A. Payment Card Industry Data Security Standard ("PCI DSS")
 B. Online Privacy Alliance
 C. TRUSTe
 D. ISO 27001

ANSWER: D. ISO 27001 specifies a management system that is intended to bring information security under explicit management control. ISO 27001 requires that management (1) systematically examine the organization's information security risks, (2) design and implement a coherent and comprehensive suite of information security controls to address those risks, and (3) adopt an overarching management process to ensure that the information security controls continue to meet the organization's information security needs on an ongoing basis. ISO 27001, unlike PCI DSS, the Online Privacy Alliance, and TRUSTe, is not an example of the self-regulatory model of data protection.

85. When should a privacy impact assessment occur?

A.   After implementation of a new project
B.   When a system holding personal information is decommissioned
C.   Before the onset of a new project and periodically thereafter
D.   Each fiscal year

ANSWER: C. A privacy impact assessment is an analysis of how information is handled to ensure handling conforms to applicable legal, regulatory, and policy requirements. An assessment should be completed before implementation of a privacy project and should be ongoing through its deployment.

86. What is an important part of a privacy impact assessment?

A.   Identifying the types of information that are to be collected
B.   Controlling access to the results of the assessment
C.   Conducting the assessment immediately after a new project is implemented
D.   Ensuring that technical safeguards are protecting all personal information

ANSWER: A. During a privacy impact assessment, the data being collected and its attributes must be closely analyzed. Specifically, what type of data is being collected, for what purpose, for how long, with whom is the data being shared, and the choices available to the data subject regarding processing should be considered.

87. Which of the following management operations are consistent with lifecycle principles?

   A.   Pseudonymize and aggregation; monitoring and enforcement
   B.   Anonymization and aggregation; archival and retrieval
   C.   Transfer and encryption; monitoring and enforcement
   D.   Management and administration; monitoring and enforcement

ANSWER: D. The information lifecycle consists of (1) collection, (2) use, (3) disclosure, and (4) retention or destruction. Associated with the information lifecycle are the management processes needed to effectively implement an organization's information privacy policies and procedures. Specifically, an organization should manage and administer any defined privacy policies while also monitoring and enforcing compliance with the policies. Without these management related activities, information cannot be adequately protected throughout its lifecycle.

88. The United States takes what approach to privacy protection?

   A.   Comprehensive
   B.   Sectoral
   C.   Co-regulatory
   D.   Self-regulatory

ANSWER: B. The United States and Japan take a sectoral approach to privacy protection in which sector specific laws are enacted as opposed to a general, more comprehensive data protection law. The EU is a notable jurisdiction with a comprehensive privacy law. Canada, Australia, and New Zealand are three major countries employing a co-regulatory model of privacy protection.

89. Which of the following is a type of administrative safeguard for personal information?

    A.   Incident response procedures
    B.   Password authentication
    C.   Locks for portable computing devices
    D.   Firewalls

ANSWER: A. Administrative safeguards are administrative actions, policies and procedures that manage the selection, development, implementation, and maintenance of security measures for protecting personal information. An incident response plan or procedure is a type of administrative safeguard. Password authentication and firewalls are types of physical safeguards, while locks are physical safeguards.

90. Which of the following is NOT a form of privacy notice?

    A.   Web pages
    B.   Icons
    C.   Signs
    D.   Product listings with prices

ANSWER: D. Privacy notices can come in many forms. In fact, any form of communication that reasonably conveys privacy related information may be used as a privacy notice. Web pages, icons, and signs are all forms of commonly used privacy notices. An organization's product listings would not constitute a privacy notice.

91. The Interactive Advertising Bureau ("IAB") uses a privacy policy in the form of what for behavior tracking?

    A.   Contract
    B.   Icon
    C.   Sign
    D.   Brochure

ANSWER: B. The IAB has developed a comprehensive self-regulatory program for online behavioral advertising. The program promotes the use of an icon and accompanying language to be displayed in or near online advertisements or on web pages where data is collected and used for behavioral advertising.

92. What are the two primary purposes of a privacy notice?

    A.   Trust and corporate accountability
    B.   Consumer education and corporate accountability
    C.   Trust and compliance
    D.   Compliance and consumer education

ANSWER: B. The primary purpose of a privacy notice is to educate the consumer about an organization's privacy practices and the options that the consumer has with respect to processing of the consumer's personal information. The secondary purpose is to hold organizations accountability for following the terms and conditions as specified in the privacy notice. If an organization fails to comply with its privacy notice, it may be held liable by the FTC for a deceptive trade practice. When companies tell consumers they will safeguard their personal information, the FTC can and does take law enforcement action to make sure that companies live up these promises.

93. Which of the following is NOT considered personal information about an employee held by the human resources department of an employer?

    A.   Sick leave requests
    B.   Salary
    C.   Title
    D.   Performance evaluations

ANSWER: C. Personal information is any information about an identified or identifiable individual. Sick leave requests, salary, and performance evaluations are typically unique to a particular person, and therefore may constitute personal information. A person's job title, on the other hand, typically is not unique, and therefore is not generally consider personal information. In other words, title is the data element least likely to uniquely identify an individual.

94. Which of the following is NOT considered personal information about a customer held by a retailer?

    A.   Order history
    B.   Voice recordings from correspondence with the customer
    C.   Purchase history
    D.   Top selling products

ANSWER: D. Personal information is any information about an identified or identifiable individual. A company's top selling products is generally derived from aggregated data that is not considered personal data. All other answers described information that would typically uniquely identify an individual and therefore is personal information.

95. Which of the following is an example of personal information from a public record in the United States?

    A.   Heath plan number from an insurance card
    B.   Name and address of an owner of a piece of real estate from a real estate deed
    C.   Driver's license number from government issued citation
    D.   Genetic information from a private genome project

ANSWER: B. Public records are information collected and maintained by the government and that are available to the public. Public records include real estate deeds, birth and marriage certificates, tax liens, and other data recorded by the government and made available for public inspection.

96. Which of the following is a privacy implication of an IPv6 internet address?

    A.   IPv6 allows for fewer IP address than its predecessor IPv4
    B.   IPv6 and IPv4 are interoperable
    C.   IPv6 is less secure than an IPv4 address
    D.   IPv6 use a new addressing scheme that may make it easier to associate an address with a specific individual

ANSWER: D. IPv6 uses a 128-bit address, allowing approximately 3.4×10^{38} addresses, or more than 7.9×10^{28} times as many addresses as IPv4, which uses only 32-bit addresses. In IPv4, the effort to conserve address space with network address translation ("NAT") helped obfuscate network address spaces, hosts, and topologies, thereby increasing privacy protection. In IPv6, however, when using address auto-configuration, the interface identifier (or MAC address) of an interface port is used to make its public IP address unique, exposing the type of hardware used and providing a unique handle for a user's online activity. Therefore, IPv6's new addressing scheme may make it easier to associate an address with a specific individual, thereby creating a privacy concern.

97. The EU Data Protection Directive uses what term to refer to sensitive personal information?

   A. Special categories of data
   B. Inherently protected data
   C. Classified data types
   D. Intrinsic data

ANSWER: A. The EU Data Protection Directive uses the term "special categories of data" to describe sensitive personal information. In accordance with the Directive, special categories of data include personal data revealing racial or ethnic origin, political opinions, religious or philosophical beliefs, trade-union membership, and the processing of data concerning health or sex life.

98. In the EU, what type of information is considered a special category of data?

   A. Country identification number
   B. Gender
   C. Political opinions
   D. Driver's license number

ANSWER: C. The EU Data Protection Directive uses the term "special categories of data" to describe sensitive personal information. In accordance with the Directive, special categories of data include personal data revealing racial or ethnic origin, political opinions, religious or philosophical beliefs, trade-union membership, and the processing of data concerning health or sex life.

99. Which type of information is considered non-personal data?

    A.   Email addresses
    B.   Gender
    C.   Salary
    D.   Aggregated Data

ANSWER: D. Personal data is any data that describes an identified or identifiable individual. "Anonymized," "de-identified," and "aggregated" data are types of non-personal data because the data generally cannot be traced back to an identified or identifiable individual.

100.   When may information about an organization be considered personal information?

    A.   When the organization is a sole proprietorship
    B.   When the organization is multi-national
    C.   When the organization files taxes
    D.   When the organization is controlled by a single Board of Director

ANSWER: A. Generally, personal information is any information describing an identified or identifiable individual (in contrast to a corporation). However, when a company is a sole proprietorship, information describing the sole proprietorship may be traceable to a specific and identifiable individual. In such cases, information about a proprietorship may be deemed personal information.

101. Which of the following may be considered personal information?

    A.   Financial data of an organization
    B.   Intellectual property of an organization
    C.   Operational data of an organization
    D.   Human resources data of an organization

ANSWER: D. Financial data, intellectual property, and operational data are all important types of information related to an organization. However, personal information is any information describing an identified or identifiable individual (in contrast to a corporation). Human resources data, on the other hand, does describe employees of an organization and therefore may constitute personal information if describing an identified or identifiable individual.

102. Which jurisdiction considers IP addresses as personal information?

    A.   Japan
    B.   Canada
    C.   EU
    D.   Australia

ANSWER: C. In the European Union, IP addresses are generally considered personal information. In fact, the Article 29 Working Party has repeatedly advised that IP addresses should be regarded as personal data, especially in those cases where the processing of IP addresses is carried out with the purpose of identifying the users of the computer.

103. Which country does not consider business contact information as personal information?

    A.   Argentina
    B.   United States
    C.   Australia
    D.   Canada

ANSWER: D. In accordance with Canada's Personal Information Protection and Electronic Documents Act ("PIPEDA"), personal information means any information about an identifiable individual, but does not include the name or business contact information of an employee of an organization.

104. Which type of personal information is almost universally considered sensitive personal information?

A. Human resources data
B. Health records
C. Name and address
D. Gender

ANSWER: B. In virtually all jurisdictions, health related data constitutes sensitive person information because it relates to the inner workings of one's body and mind.

105. Which characteristic of cloud computing provides computer services such as email, applications, network or server service without requiring human interaction with each service provider?

A. Broad network access
B. On-demand
C. Resource pooling
D. Rapid elasticity

ANSWER: B. On-demand self-service refers to the ability to access computing resources in the cloud without having to first interact with the cloud provider. Broad network access is the ability to connect to the cloud through a network using standard mechanisms employed on a wide range of devices. Resource pooling refers to aggregation of computing resources for use by many cloud consumers. Rapid elasticity is a provider's ability to automatically provision cloud resources. Finally, measured service refers to provider's ability to measure, control, and report computing resource usage so as to provide transparency for both the provider and consumer of the cloud. On-demand self-service, broad network access, resource pooling, rapid elasticity, and measured service are all characteristics of cloud computing.

106. In which service model of cloud computing do users rent space in a virtual data center and other resources, such as computing and network capability?

    A.   Infrastructure as a service ("IaaS")
    B.   Platform as a service ("PaaS")
    C.   Software as a service ("SaaS")
    D.   Network as a service ("NaaS")

ANSWER: A. IaaS is the most basic cloud service model. In IaaS, users rent computing resources, such as storage, network capacity, and processing power from cloud providers. The cloud provider owns the equipment and is responsible for housing, running, and maintaining it. Under PaaS, cloud providers deliver a computing platform, typically including an operating system, database, and web server. Web developers build and publish web applications using the platform. Finally, with SaaS, applications are hosted by the cloud vendor in the cloud. Customers typically access the applications through a web browser over the Internet. SaaS is often referred to as "on-demand software."

107. What practice have major search engines recently employed to address privacy concerns over search data retained by the search engines?

    A.   Search engines are no longer storing search history data for any of their users
    B.   Search engines are deleting search data after one year from the search
    C.   Search engines are deleting search data after notification from the government
    D.   Search engines are anonymizing search data after a predetermined period of time

ANSWER: D. A user's browsing history is an important asset to a search engine company. Therefore, search companies would not readily agree to permanently deleting this data. Instead, they have taken the middle ground by anonymizing search data (including page views, page clicks, ad views, and ad clicks) after a predetermined period of time (ranging from 90 days to 24 months).

108.   Which type of cookie is used to remember a user's login credentials between visits to a particular website?

A.   First party cookie
B.   Persistent cookie
C.   Third party cookie
D.   Session cookie

ANSWER: B. Persistent cookies, unlike session cookies, remain stored on the user's computer for a predetermined period and persistent beyond a user's session. For example, if a persistent cookie has its "Max-Age" set to 1 year, then within the year, the initial value set in that cookie would be sent back to the server every time the user visits the server. Therefore, persistent cookies enable features like the "remember me" authentication functionality.

109.   The EU Cookie Directive established what new principle?

A.   Website operators are required to provide website users the opportunity to opt-out from the use of cookies
B.   Website operators are required to provide website users written notice that a cookie is placed on the user's device upon leaving the website
C.   Website operators are requires to obtain the user's consent before placing a cookie on the user's device
D.   Cookies are classified as sensitive personal information

ANSWER: C. The EU Cookie Directive requires a user's consent before cookies may be placed on the user's computer. Consent is defined as "any freely given specific and informed indication of his wishes by which the data subject signifies his agreement to personal data relating to him being processed."

110. The Digital Advertising Alliance has recently developed an icon program for what purpose?

 A. To develop effective self-regulatory principles for online behavioral advertising
 B. To prevent websites from using first-party cookies
 C. To create a set of procedures for increasing an advertising campaign's return on investment
 D. To combat unsolicited electronic mail

ANSWER: A. The Digital Advertising Alliance ("DAA") Self-Regulatory Program for Online Behavioral Advertising was launched in 2010. The DAA includes a consortium of the nation's largest media and marketing associations, including the American Association of Advertising Agencies (4A's), the Association of National Advertisers (ANA), the American Advertising Federation (AAF), the Direct Marketing Association (DMA), the Interactive Advertising Bureau (IAB), and the Network Advertising Initiative (NAI). These associations and their thousands of members are committed to developing effective self-regulatory solutions to consumer choice in online behavioral advertising (OBA). Based on the seven self-regulatory principles for online behavioral advertising proposed by the Federal Trade Commission, the DAA program is designed to give consumers enhanced control over the collection and use of data regarding their Internet viewing for OBA purposes.

111. TRUSTe, WebTrust, and BBBOnline are organizations that offer what?

 A. Online security initiatives
 B. Third party authentication services
 C. Web-based cloud computing platforms
 D. Industry self-regulatory seal programs

ANSWER: D. TRUSTe, WebTrust, and BBBOnline all offer self-regulatory seal programs dealing with online privacy.

112.   Which web form input technique should be used in
        accordance with information security and privacy best
        practices?

    A.   Scrolling text box
    B.   One-line text box
    C.   Check box for acknowledgement of a privacy policy
    D.   Radio button for acknowledgement of a privacy policy

ANSWER: C. Information security and privacy best practices
dictate that a user's acknowledgement of an organization's privacy
policy be indicated through the use of a check box. Check boxes
allow for both opt-in and opt-out choice, which is routinely provided
for in a privacy policy. Text boxes, on the other hand, are inherently
less secure than check boxes and radio buttons because the user's
input is not restricted. This lack of control over the user's input
creates a potential security issue when using text boxes. Radio
buttons are not recommended for acknowledgement of a privacy
policy because once a radio button is selected, it generally cannot be
unselected by the user.

113.   Which of the following is a common criticism of privacy
        notices?

    A.   Layered privacy notices are confusing and overly
          complex
    B.   Privacy notices are often written in legalese and difficult
          to understand
    C.   Privacy policies are not required for most websites that
          collect personal information
    D.   The short notice in a layered privacy notice does not
          provide a complete disclosure of a company's privacy
          policies

ANSWER: B. The original goal of a privacy notice was to create
transparency in an organization's data collection practices and to
help users make informed decisions. Unfortunately, most users do
not read privacy notices because they are drafted in a verbose and
legally formalistic manner that is difficult to understand. Layered
privacy notices address this concern by presenting the user with a
short notice that is simple and concise. The short notice

summarizes the organization's information handling practices and the choices available to users. The full privacy notice is typically accessible by a hyperlink from the short notice in case the user wants more information about the organization's privacy practices.

114.   What is NOT a risk associated with spyware?

    A.   Spyware may enable access to resources that a user would otherwise not be able to access
    B.   Spyware may collect sensitive personal information such as bank account numbers and passwords
    C.   Spyware may slow a computer system down and prevent normal operation of the system
    D.   Spyware may track a user's online activity and send it to remote parties

ANSWER: A. Spyware is software that gathers information about a person or organization without their knowledge and that may send such information to another entity without the person's consent. Spyware may also assert control over a computer without the owner's knowledge. Spyware is generally classified into four types: (1) system monitors, (2) Trojans, (3) adware, and (4) tracking cookies. Spyware presents many risks to the security of an organization's informational assets and systems. Spyware does not have the ability to grant a user access to a resource that the user is not authorized to access. Software that provides a user with access to a resource that the user is not authorized to access would generally be called an "exploit" and not spyware.

115.   Which of the following is a standard protocol for the secure the transmission of personal information over the Internet?

    A.   P3P
    B.   TCP
    C.   SSL
    D.   IP addresses

ANSWER: C. Transport layer security ("TLS") and its predecessor, secure sockets layer ("SSL"), are cryptographic protocols that provide secure communications over the Internet. Several versions of TLS and SSL are in widespread use in Internet applications such as web browsing, email, Internet faxing, instant messaging, and voice-over-IP ("VoIP").

116. Which of the following is a type of social engineering?

    A.   The use of key loggers to record usernames and passwords
    B.   Injecting malicious code into a third-party website
    C.   Brute force password attacks
    D.   The use of non-technical means to gain access to restricted information

ANSWER: D. Social engineering, in the context of information security, refers to the psychological (i.e., not-technical) manipulation of people with the goal of having those people perform actions or divulge confidential information.

117. Which of the following is NOT a requirement for management of an organization under ISO 27001?

    A.   Systematically examine the organization's information security risks
    B.   Design and implement a coherent and comprehensive suite of information security controls to address risks
    C.   Adopt an overarching management process to ensure that information security controls continue to meet the organization's information security needs on an ongoing basis
    D.   Communicate information security policies and best practices to all employees of an organization

ANSWER: D. ISO 27001 specifies a management system that is intended to bring information security under explicit management control. ISO 27001 requires that management (1) systematically examine the organization's information security risks, (2) design and implement a coherent and comprehensive suite of information security controls to address those risks, and (3) adopt an overarching management process to ensure that the information security controls continue to meet the organization's information security needs on an ongoing basis. While it is a good practice to communicate information security policies to all employees, it is not a practice specified by ISO 27001.

118.   What two technologies may be used to describe, create, and transport content online?

A.   HTML and TCP
B.   HTML and XML
C.   HTML and SSL
D.   HTML and URL

ANSWER: B. Hypertext Markup Language ("HTML") and eXtensible Markup Language ("XML") are two technologies used to describe, create, and transport online content. XML is a markup language designed to transport and store data, while HTML is a markup language designed to render and display data.

119.   Which of the following is NOT a best practice for information security audits?

A.   Information security policies and procedures must be in conformance with the organization's published policy and comply with all applicable laws and regulations
B.   An organization must complete an audit of its storage and processing procedures on a regular basis
C.   The audit must be conducted by an independent third-party
D.   Results of the audit must be analyzed and plans should be formulated to remediate any deficiencies

ANSWER: C. Although information security audits may be conducted by third-parties, it is not a requirement. Audits may be performed using in-house personnel. All other statements are best practices for information security audits. Specifically, audits must be in compliance with the organization's policies, as well as all applicable laws and regulations. Audits must also be completed at regular intervals to ensure deficiencies are identified in a timely manner. Finally, results of audits must be analyzed and deficiencies remediated.

120. What is the second step of information security incident management and the step immediately after discovery of a security breach?

A. Containment
B. Prevention
C. Eradication
D. Notification

ANSWER: A. When an information security incident does occur, an organization must know how to appropriately respond. The basic incident management and response process includes (1) incident discovery, (2) containment and analysis, (3) notification, and (4) eradication and future prevention.

121. A security log should record which events?

A. Valid logins and invalid login attempts
B. Database errors
C. Application errors
D. Device driver failure

ANSWER: A. A security log is used to track security-related information on a computer system. The log typically contains records of login/logout activity and other security-related events specified by the system's audit policy. Other types of logs include application logs and system logs. A system log contains events that are logged by the operating system and its components. An application log records events that are triggered by the applications used on a computer system. Events that are written to the application log are determined by the developers of the software program, not the operating system.

122. Which of the following accurately describes the use of digital signatures to secure an email

    A. Sender uses recipient's public key and receiver uses his public key
    B. Sender uses sender's private key and receiver uses sender's public key
    C. Sender uses recipient's private key and receiver uses his public key
    D. Sender uses recipient's public key and receiver uses his private key

ANSWER: B. Public-key cryptography (also called asymmetric-key cryptography) uses a pair of keys to encrypt and decrypt content. Each user has a pair of cryptographic keys – a public encryption key and a private decryption key. The public key is widely distributed, while the private key is known only to its owner. The keys are related mathematically, but the parameters used to generate the keys are chosen so that calculating the private key from the public key is virtually impossible. The use of the keys is slightly different when authenticating content for digital signatures. With digital signatures, the sender uses his private key to digitally sign the message. The recipient uses the sender's public key, along with the message and digital signature, to confirm that the message is authentic.

123. The principle of segregation is designed to prevent which of the following security threats?

    A. A user having access to a company's sensitive personal information
    B. An administrator from disabling the account of another administrator
    C. A single user from having complete access to perform an essential function
    D. A user having access to confidential information that he does not need to know

ANSWER: C. Segregation, or separation of duties, is a classic security method to manage conflicts of interest and fraud. It restricts the amount of power held by any one individual, thereby placing barrier to prevent fraud. Generally, segregation prevents a single user from having complete access to perform an essential function, such as paying an invoice.

124. Which of the following accurately describes public-key cryptography ("PKI")?

A. Content is encrypted with a shared key and decrypted with a private key
B. Content is encrypted with a public key and decrypted with a private key
C. Content is encrypted with a public key and decrypted with a public key
D. Content is encrypted with a private key and decrypted with a private key

ANSWER: B. Public-key cryptography (also called asymmetric-key cryptography) uses a pair of keys to encrypt and decrypt content. Each user has a pair of cryptographic keys – a public encryption key and a private decryption key. The public key is widely distributed, while the private key is known only to its owner. The keys are related mathematically, but the parameters used to generate the keys are chosen so that calculating the private key from the public key is virtually impossible.

125. Which of the following is correct about authentication schemes for computer access?

A. Most schemes rely solely on password authentication
B. Passcard authentication does not increase security when used in conjunction with passwords
C. Biometric authentication can be easily circumvented
D. Out of band authentication scheme are a type of one-factor authentication

ANSWER: A. Although two-factor authentication schemes drastically increase security, most website still rely on password only authentication. Two-factor authentication is a security process in which the user provides two means of identification, one of which is typically a physical token, such as a card, and the other of which is typically something memorized, such as a security code or password. In this context, the two factors involved are sometimes referred to as something you have (e.g., a passcard) and something you know (e.g., a password).

126.   Information security generally balances the risk of loss of an asset with the cost of what two factors?

    A.   Intrusion detection systems and instruction prevention systems
    B.   Security protection and security management
    C.   Security controls and storage of the asset
    D.   Replacement of the asset and storage of the asset

ANSWER: B. With respect to information security, the risk of loss is balanced with the costs of providing security to prevent loss. Security generally consists of security protection and security management (that is, the security policy and controls and the people used to implement and manage the policy and controls).

127.   A robust information classification scheme enables what?

    A.   A clearer privacy notice
    B.   Test controls to detect unauthorized access
    C.   Increases in computing efficiency
    D.   A basis for managing access to informational assets

ANSWER: D. Information classification is an important part of managing access to informational assets. Generally information may be classified as either public, confidential, and/or sensitive. Depending on the classification, access should be restricted to only those persons with a need to know the information (also known as role-based access control).

128. Information security systems should be designed with what two core competing goals in mind?

A. Minimum necessary controls and ease of use
B. Protecting information and restricting access to information
C. Protecting information and providing access to information
D. Restricting access to information and encrypting information

ANSWER: C. A general principle when designing an information security system is that one must balance protecting information with the need to provide access to the information. These are the two primary objectives when formulating an information security system or policy.

129. Which one of the following is NOT a purpose of the APEC Privacy Framework, which was approved by APEC ministers in 2004?

A. Improve information sharing among government agencies and regulators
B. Establish a common set of privacy principles
C. Encourage the use of electronic data as a means to enhance and expand business
D. Promote the use of automated encryption mechanisms for sensitive data

ANSWER: D. The Asia-Pacific Economic Cooperation ("APEC") Privacy Framework, which is consistent with the OECD's 1980 Guidelines, has the following primary goals: (1) improve information sharing among government agencies and regulators, (2) facilitate the safe transfer of information between economies, (3) establish a common set of privacy principles, (4) encourage the use of electronic data as a means to enhance and expand business, and (5) provide technical assistance to those economies that have yet to address privacy from a regulatory or policy perspective.

130. What are the most common and important class of security control?

    A.   Preventive
    B.   Corrective
    C.   Detective
    D.   Remedial

ANSWER: A. Preventive controls are designed to protect information before a security event occurs, and therefore are the most important and common. Examples of preventive controls include firewalls, passwords, and encryption. Detective controls are designed to detect a security event. Examples of detective controls include security logs and intrusion detection systems. Finally, corrective controls are designed to protect information after a security event occurs. Examples of corrective controls include intrusion preventive systems that automatically block suspicious activity. More than one type of control may be used to protect information. For example, confidential information should be protected by several controls of varying classes. Information of lower importance, such as public information, may be protected by fewer controls or even no controls.

131. The information security department at an organization should communicate information security policies to whom?

    A.   The information security and privacy groups responsible for the data related to the policies
    B.   All employees that use data related to the policies
    C.   Executives and managers in the organization
    D.   All employees of the organization

ANSWER: D. Information security policies should be communicated to all employees and not just to the security and privacy professionals at an organization. Every employee plays a part in protecting an organization's information, even those employees without computer access. For example, a janitor may leave a door unlocked, which in turn allows an intruder to remove a computer containing personal information. Therefore, all employees should be aware of information security policies.

132. What are the main sources of requirements for information security policies?

   A.   Organization needs and customer's demands
   B.   Customer requests and manager feedback
   C.   Relevant laws and an organization's privacy policy
   D.   Standards and privacy policies

ANSWER: C. The main sources of requirements for information security policies come from applicable laws, rules, and regulations, as well as from an organization's privacy policy. Although customer complaints and requests may be considered when developing an information security policy, they are not a main source and inclusion would be optional and not required.

133. What is the step of information security incident management after containment of a security breach?

   A.   Containment
   B.   Prevention
   C.   Analysis
   D.   Notification

ANSWER: D. When an information security incident does occur, an organization must know how to appropriately respond. The basic incident management and response process includes (1) incident discovery, (2) containment and analysis, (3) notification, and (4) eradication and future prevention.

134. Which of the following is an industry standard formula for assessing risk?

   A.   Risk = Threat x Vulnerability x Expected Loss
   B.   Risk = Control / Threat x Vulnerability
   C.   Risk = Threat + Vulnerability − Expected Loss
   D.   Risk = Threat x Vulnerability / Control

ANSWER: A. As indicated by the correct formula, the risk associated with an organization's information technology is directly related to three parameters: (1) threats, (2) vulnerabilities, and (3) expected loss. Threats are any circumstances that may cause an undesirable event, such as a data breach. Vulnerabilities are weaknesses in an organization's information systems, policies, or procedures. When a threat exploits some vulnerability, a security event that causes risk occurs. The amount of the risk for a particular security event is equal to the probability of the event occurring times the expected loss associated with the event. Answers B – D provide incorrect formulations of risk.

135.   In addition to threats and vulnerabilities, what other factor should be considered when evaluating risk?

   A.   Controls
   B.   Expected Loss
   C.   Technical safeguards
   D.   Likelihood of system failure

ANSWER: B. The risk associated with an organization's information technology is directly related to three parameters: (1) threats, (2) vulnerabilities, and (3) expected loss.

136.   Which of the following is NOT a major source of security requirements for an organization?

   A.   Legal and regulatory obligations
   B.   The organization's privacy policy
   C.   Contractual obligations
   D.   Customer complaints and evaluations

ANSWER: D. Legal, regulatory, and contractual obligations are all primary sources of security requirements for an organization. An organization's privacy policy is also another major source of security requirements. Customer complaints and evaluations, on the other hand, are not a primary source. Addressing customer complaints would typically be optional and not a requirement.

137.	In accordance with information security best practices, which employees of an organization are responsible for information security?

A.	Information security personnel
B.	All managers
C.	All employees
D.	The executive team

ANSWER: C. While information security personnel can perform a wide range of tasks related to information security at an organization, ultimately all employees are responsible for ensuring information security. Accordingly, all employees should be trained in information handling best practices.

138.	Which of the following is one of the first steps when establishing an information security program?

A.	Monitor the security programs
B.	Identify and evaluate risks
C.	Define the security policy
D.	Review complaints and evaluations

ANSWER: C. Generally, an information security program should be established by (1) defining the security policy and security management system; (2) identifying and evaluating any risks, (3) selecting appropriate controls to address the identified risks, and (4) obtaining management approval of program, and (5) monitoring and reviewing compliance with the program.

139.	What type of log should record a device driver that fails to load properly?

A.	Security log
B.	System log
C.	Application log
D.	Device log

ANSWER: B. A system log contains events that are logged by the operating system and its components, such as device drivers. An application log records events that are triggered by the applications used on a computer system, such as a database application. Events that are written to the application log are determined by the developers of the software program, not the operating system. A security log is used to track security-related information on a computer system. The log typically contains records of login/logout activity and other security-related events specified by the system's audit policy.

140. In which country is express authorization from the data protection authority required for the automatic processing of biometric data?

   A.   France
   B.   Australia
   C.   Canada
   D.   United States

ANSWER: A. In France, express authorization must be obtained from the Commission nationale de l'informatique et des libertés (the "CNIL") before the automatic processing of biometric data.

141. Which of the following is NOT a principle set forth in the Guidelines on the Protection of Privacy and Transborder Flows of Personal Data adopted by the Organization for Economic Cooperation and Development in 1980 ("OECD Guidelines")?

   A.   Data Quality
   B.   Collection Limitation
   C.   Openness
   D.   Adequate Protection

ANSWER: D. The eight principles contained in the OECD guidelines are: (1) collection limitation principles, (2) data quality principle, (3) purpose specification principle, (4) use limitation principle, (5) security safeguards principle, (6) openness principle, (7) individual participation principle, and (8) accountability principle.

142. What are the primary goals EU Data Protection Directive?

A. Reduce piracy and discourage international transfers of personal information
B. Safeguard the fundamental right of privacy and enable the free flow of personal information among member states
C. Encourage international transfers of personal information and safeguarding users on online websites
D. Safeguarding the fundamental right of privacy and protecting children from the illegal collection of personal information

ANSWER: B. Article 3 of the EU Data Protection Directive indicates that its main goals are (1) safeguarding the fundamental right of privacy and (2) enabling the free flow of personal information among member states.

143. Who is responsible for protecting informational assets at an organization?

A. All employees, vendors, and consultants
B. Employees in the information security department
C. Managers
D. The chief executive officer

ANSWER: A. While information security personnel can perform a wide range of tasks related to information security at an organization, it is every employees' responsibility to protect informational assets. Information security is ultimately about people. Vendors and consultants should always be informed of information security policies and procedures if they are given access to information.

144. Which of the following is NOT a privacy principle of the Safe Harbor program developed by the Department of Commerce in consultation with the European Commission?

   A. Notice
   B. Choice
   C. Access
   D. Respect

ANSWER: D. The European Union ("EU") Data Protection Directive prohibits the transfer of personal data to non-European Union countries that do not meet the European Union (EU) "adequacy" standard for privacy protection. While the United States and the EU share the goal of enhancing privacy protection for their citizens, the United States takes a different approach to privacy from that taken by the EU. The U.S. Department of Commerce in consultation with the European Commission developed the Safe Harbor framework to bridge these differences in approach and provide a streamlined means for U.S. organizations to comply with the Directive. Organizations desiring to join the program must comply with the seven Safe Harbor privacy principles, which are (1) notice, (2) choice, (3) onward transfer to third parties, (4) access, (5) security, (6) data integrity, and (7) enforcement.

145. Which of the following is NOT a principle of privacy by design?

   A. Visibility and transparency
   B. Privacy as the default setting
   C. Equal treatment of data
   D. End to end security

ANSWER: C. The Information and Privacy Commissioner of Ontario, Canada developed the privacy by design framework in the 1990s. It includes the following seven principles: (1) Proactive not Reactive; Preventative not Remedial; (2) Privacy as the Default Setting; (3) Privacy Embedded into Design, (4) Full Functionality — Positive-Sum, not Zero-Sum; (5) End-to-End Security — Full Lifecycle Protection; (6)Visibility and Transparency — Keep it Open; and (7) Respect for User Privacy — Keep it User-Centric.

146. Which of the following accurately describes an organization's ability to monitor its employees in the EU?

A. Employee monitoring is never permitted
B. Employee monitoring is permitted only within common area that are owned by the organization
C. Employee monitoring is permitted only with the express verbal consent of the employee
D. Personal data processed in connection with the monitoring must be adequate, relevant, and not excessive

ANSWER: D. Once an employer decides to monitor an employee, the Article 29 Working Party suggests that the organization follow the following seven basic principles: (1) an employer must determine whether the monitoring is absolutely necessary for the specified purpose, (2) data collected through the monitoring must respond to a "specified, explicit and legitimate" purpose and cannot be processed for a different purpose, (3) the employer must provide clear and open notice to employees about the monitoring, (4) employers may monitor only to safeguard their legitimate interests, while not violating an employee's fundamental rights, (5) personal data processed in connection with the monitoring must be adequate, relevant, and not excessive, (6) personal data must be updated and retained only for the period deemed necessary for the purpose to be achieved, and (7) the employer must implement all appropriate technical and organizational measures to ensure that any personal data is protected from alteration, unauthorized access, and misuse.

147.   Which of the following is NOT an exception to the EU Data
        Protection Directive's requirement that transfers of personal
        data may only be made to third countries which ensure an
        adequate level of protection?

   A.   The transfer complies with all applicable laws of the
         receiving country
   B.   The transfer is necessary for the performance of a
         contract between the data subject and the controller
   C.   The transfer is necessary in order to protect the vital
         interests of the data subject
   D.   The transfer is necessary or legally required on important
         public interest grounds

ANSWER: A. Article 26(1) of the EU Data Protection Directive
states that transfers of personal data to a third country which do not
ensure an adequate level of protection may take place if the data
subject has "given his consent unambiguously to the proposed
transfer." Other exceptions include: (1) the transfer is necessary for
the performance of a contract between the data subject and the
controller, (2) the transfer is necessary for the conclusion or
performance of a contract concluded in the interest of the data
subject, (3) the transfer is necessary or legally required on important
public interest grounds, and (4) the transfer is necessary in order to
protect the vital interests of the data subject. B–D set forth valid
exceptions.

148.   Which of the following may be classified as a deceptive trade
        practice by the FTC?

   A.   A website's privacy notice clearly states that it will not
         encrypt sensitive personal information, and the website
         does not in fact encrypt the data
   B.   An organization promises to honor opt-out requests
         within 10 days but fails to honor opt-out requests.
   C.   A rogue employee steals credit card information even
         though the organization took reasonable precautions to
         protect the credit card information
   D.   A bank does not comply with a regulation prohibiting the
         bank from revealing information about its customers

ANSWER: B. If an organization fails to comply with its privacy notice, it may be held liable by the FTC for a deceptive trade practice under Section 5 of the FTC Act, which prohibits "unfair or deceptive acts or practices in or affecting commerce." When companies tell consumers they will safeguard their personal information, the FTC can and does take law enforcement action to make sure that companies live up these promises. A violation of a promise made in a privacy notice is an example of a deceptive trade practice. Answer A would be an example of an unfair trade practice. The organization is not being deceptive but the potential harm caused by the website's failure to encrypt sensitive data clearly outweighs the cost of providing encryption, a commonplace and inexpensive security control. Answer C would not be a deceptive trade practice because the organization had reasonable security measures, and the employee simply committed a crime. Answer D is incorrect because the FTC has no jurisdiction over banks and common carriers, which are under the supervision of other governmental agencies.

149. Which of the following is NOT a common category of information used when developing information security controls?

A. Public
B. Sensitive
C. Confidential
D. Personal

ANSWER: D. The most common information classification scheme divides information into three categories: (1) public information, (2) sensitive information, and (3) confidential information. Public information by its very nature is designed to be shared broadly, without restriction. Examples of public information include marketing material, press releases, and regulatory reports submitted to government agencies. Sensitive information is considered internal and should not be released outside of an organization. Examples of sensitive information include business plans, financial data, and documents reflecting corporate strategy. Confidential information is generally intended for a very specific purpose and should not be disclosed to anyone without a demonstrated need to know. Examples of confidential information include employee bank account information, social security numbers, and login credentials (e.g., username and password).

150.   What is the first step of information security incident management?

    A.   Prevention
    B.   Containment
    C.   Analysis
    D.   Discovery

ANSWER: D. When an information security incident does occur, an organization must know how to appropriately respond. The basic incident management and response process includes (1) incident discovery, (2) containment and analysis, (3) notification, and (4) eradication and future prevention.